THE MODERN APE

BY MARY BELL

A BRIEF, CRITICAL NARRATIVE

ISBN

Hardcover: 978-1-967616-19-0
Paperback: 978-1-967616-20-6

Contents

Disclaimer

If you are a member of those sensitive groups who are easily triggered, do not read this narrative. Stop here and go back. Some information stated in this narrative might be offensive to certain individuals. I am not responsible for anyone's behavior or feelings occurring after they have read this narrative. You are big boys and girls, and you are responsible for yourselves. Therefore, you have been warned.

"By the authority vested in me as President by the Constitution and the laws of the United States of America, and section 301 of title 3, United States Code, it is hereby ordered as follows:

Section 1. Purpose. The First Amendment to the United States Constitution, an amendment essential to the success of our Republic, enshrines the right of the American people to speak freely in the public square without Government interference. Over the last 4 years, the previous administration trampled free speech rights by censoring Americans' speech on online platforms, often by exerting substantial coercive pressure on third parties, such as social media companies, to moderate, deplatform, or otherwise suppress speech that the Federal Government did not approve. Under the guise of combatting "misinformation," "disinformation," and "misinformation," the Federal Government infringed on the constitutionally protected speech rights of American citizens across the United States in a manner that advanced the Government's preferred narrative about significant matters of public debate. Government censorship of speech is intolerable in a free society.

Sec. 2. Policy. It is the policy of the United States to:

(a) secure the right of the American people to engage in constitutionally protected speech;

(b) ensure that no Federal Government officer, employee, or agent engages in or facilitates any conduct that would unconstitutionally abridge the free speech of any American citizen;

(c) ensure that no taxpayer resources are used to engage in or facilitate any conduct that would unconstitutionally abridge the free speech of any American citizen, and

(d) identify and take appropriate action to correct past misconduct by the Federal Government related to censorship of protected speech.

Sec. 3. Ending Censorship of Protected Speech.

(a) No Federal department, agency, entity, officer, employee, or agent may act or use any Federal resources in a manner contrary to section 2 of this order.

(b) The Attorney General, in consultation with the heads of executive departments and agencies, shall investigate the activities of the Federal Government over the last 4 years that are inconsistent with the purposes and policies of this order and prepare a report to be submitted to the President, through the Deputy Chief of Staff for Policy, with recommendations for appropriate remedial actions to be taken based on the findings of the report.

Sec. 4. General Provisions. (a) Nothing in this order shall be construed to impair or otherwise affect:

(i) the authority granted by law to an executive department or agency, or the head thereof; or

(ii) the functions of the Director of the Office of Management and Budget relating to budgetary, administrative, or legislative proposals.

(b) This order shall be implemented consistent with applicable law and subject to the availability of appropriations.

(c) This order is not intended to, and does not, create any right or benefit, substantive or procedural, enforceable at law or in equity by any party against the United States, its departments, agencies, or entities, its officers, employees, or agents, or any other person."

Restoring Freedom Of Speech And Ending Federal Censorship – The White House

Preface

"Humans are classified in the sub-group of primates known as the Great Apes.

Humans are primates and are classified along with all other apes in a primate sub-group known as the hominoids (Superfamily Hominoidea).

This ape group can be further subdivided into the Great Apes and Lesser Apes. Humans have bodies that are genetically and structurally very similar to those of the Great Apes, and so we are classified in the Great Apes sub-group, which is also known as the hominids (Family Hominidae).

The Great Apes are named for their large bodies. They also have larger brains than other primates. Like Lesser Apes, the Great Apes are active during the day. There are four types of Great Apes – the orangutans, gorillas, chimpanzees and humans.

There is only one living species of human – Modern Humans, Homo sapiens. Humans now live in almost every part of the world."

Humans and Other Great Apes - The Australian Museum

About The Author

Mary Bell is a humor & investigative writer who has authored the book, "The Rat," by Mary Bell. She has worked in the healthcare & social services industries for over 20 years. Her insight has helped thousands of people throughout her years. Her goal of this narrative is to inspire, challenge, intrigue, and entertain you with her broad scope of the many issues facing our world today, especially in the United States of America. She is a proud American who is a natural-born leader seeking to "be the change" in a world that seems resistant.

HealthScare

My times working in the healthcare and social services industries were some of the most miserable times during my adult life. It was draining, depressing, hard work for no money, laborious, not worth my time, and traumatic. I do not recommend anyone to do these grueling jobs taking care of people. There is not enough incentive for people to work in these industries. Even working in customer service is awful. I find people to be big babies, whiny, feeling entitled, too needy, and ungrateful towards those who receive very little in exchange for tolerating the worst bullshit in the world. How does that bring peace? All the meditation in the world won't do shit to combat the disgusting, greedy human primate who "suckles on your teats until you have sore, chapped nipples" (Ron Swanson from Parks & Recreation). Anyway, back to helping the lousy primate commonly referred to as "the human ape." Helping people is overrated, and I regret helping the sick and dying. In my opinion, some people shouldn't be here. We shouldn't keep certain folks alive. Why? So, they suffer, and we suffer? Why add to suffering? Why not promote peace and harmony and eliminate those who don't contribute to peace and harmony? Or at least prevent the possibility of someone like this from existing.

Believe it or not, I'm a nice person, and I've heard constantly from my former clients how much they would rather have me take care of them than anyone else. They all raved about me. Little did they know, I couldn't stand this job, but I did it so well. So well, all my co-workers were jealous, especially all the women. God forbid I should be gentle with those who were in weak, vulnerable positions. I mean, I've been in those positions. I treated them as I wished to be treated when in a crappy situation (Do unto others as you wish to be done to you. Remember?). That's very nice of me. I'm not adding more bad karma to my karmic cycle belt. I could have been like everyone else and abused those who were suffering. Believe me, there were many abusive healthcare workers. All were females. I will always remember these females taunting this old woman who had Alzheimer's, and I came to the rescue to comfort this elderly resident. Unlike these chicks, I took the higher road, and I received very little in return. I want a gold medal for that. Nah, palladium.

Wiping dirty, shitty ass for a living is one of the top worst jobs in the world. It's not just the actual shit that's gross. It's also the emotional drain an indolent person can cause you. Being a professional caregiver is not for the faint of heart, and it's the most underpaid and underappreciated position in the healthcare and social services industries. Professional caregivers should be paid what you people think your lives are worth. Is your life worth only 12.00 an hour, to you? Then you will receive 12.00 an hour's care. Good luck with that. People act like caregivers should be like saints 24/7 when there is so much we must deal with daily. Are you 100% perfect at your job 100% of the time? Of course not. Do not expect us to be either, especially since our jobs are a lot harder than yours. It's not just the people who must care for them in this industry; it's the business and the state governments who frequently get in the way of care. We must do everything in our power to not lose our jobs, even if that means sacrificing good care for our loved ones. Don't blame us. Blame your legislators. Healthcare in the United States is operated and treated as a business, and it shouldn't be. Because it's treated as a business, the primary concern is profit, not people. Your loved ones do not matter in this industry. Your loved ones are a means to an end, and that end is MONEY. So, next time you criticize a CNA, a nurse, or even a laundry person in the nursing home where your mother resides, remember there is always someone at the top of the pyramid calling the shots. We low-wage, simple minions on the bottom have little, if any, say about how a facility is managed. Everyone knows this. If you can do better, I suggest you wipe your mother's shitty ass yourself, 24/7. Oh, and don't forget to learn about blood-borne pathogens, CPR, medication administration, diagnoses, PMT procedures, First Aid for adults, your legal rights and responsibilities as a caregiver in your state, proper medical documentation and jargon, Epidemiology, Pathology, Human Development, the process of aging and dying, abnormal psychology, Autism Spectrum Disorder, mental illness, the list goes on.

Sometimes, our patients, residents, and/or clients have violent behaviors. It is illegal, at least in blue states, to medicate them so that they basically calm down and stay still; it's also illegal to use restraints. There are many violent clients we must deal with, and some of these clients might become injured when you fight back to defend your life. It is a normal human reaction to fight. People will be injured. The state doesn't care. You lose your job and your license and possibly go to jail. Some employees have become disabled, unable to work ever again because of these violent clients. There have even been employees who have been killed taking care of these primates. There are no consequences for these violent primates for hurting others, but there are consequences for us to do what we should be doing in a crisis. Make that make sense. During the heat of the moment, you're not always going to use your PMT skills (Physical Management Training); it's normal to do what it takes to survive when you're being attacked. I remember a pregnant coworker of mine got fired for defending her baby against a retarded, violent client. The managers, all female, were negligent in giving my coworker a violent client to take care of, knowing my coworker was pregnant. The managers were incompetent, and they should have given that violent client to a man instead. Men are very much needed in this industry to contain aggressive male patients, clients, or residents physically. Even some female clients are tough and scary. These people are out of their minds, they have no sense at all, they need better management than this, and medicating them, at least,

3

would be a great idea, so they calm down. We went from one extreme to the next in this country. To crazy abuse, to anything goes with no standards. And you wonder why there is a high turnover in this industry and industries like it. Your democrats do not care at all about increasing wages for these professionals, nor do they care to make working conditions better. Democrats are known for pretending to care about the little person, on paper, but in practice, Dumbocrats do much harm to society. My state alone is a great example of that, and later in this narrative, you will see more examples.

HealthScare Continued

I do not know why I decided to become a CNA back in 2002, but I think I saw how a position was where there was a great need for caregivers. I had thought about going into nursing, but I never did pursue that route. I don't know why I didn't; part of me regrets not pursuing a career in nursing because it's such a lucrative field, and one can do so much in this field, from acute care to consulting and even teaching. In addition, I would have retired by age 40. Well, when you're young, you're young and dumb. I also thought, at the time, "I'm not gonna do this job for long." I was wrong. There is a lot of discord within this industry and a lot of corruption. I guess pretty much everything in this country is corrupt; shameful healthcare must be one of those things. During my CNA training, our nurse instructor, who I thought was such a raging, old bitch, said two things that I will never forget. One thing she said, I agreed, and the other, I did not agree. One thing she said was that in HealthScare (the American Healthcare industry) it's "Profit before people." It was true for her many moons ago, and it was true for me throughout my time working as a professional caregiver. It is also true today. The other thing she said, which I did not agree with then and do not agree with now, is "It's a privilege to take care of someone." Bitch, what?? Now, don't get me wrong, you can learn a lot about life, mortality, etc., from taking care of a sick person, but it is NOT a privilege for the caregiver. It is and always will be a privilege for the one being cared for. It is a privilege, not a right, to have someone put up with you, wipe your smelly ass, and deal with your crazy, violent behavior. One should feel grateful for the care, and your loved ones should feel grateful, too. If you're not grateful for those who bust their asses for you and your loved ones getting paid in peanuts, then I recommend you do the job yourselves. The other option is to shut your mouth and don't bitch. Guess what? Caregivers are still in need, and it's a revolving door in this industry and industries like it. Why?

Because this job is horrible and there's no money in it. Incredibly high turnover, low wages, no respect for caregivers, we are blamed for everything, and if you have any integrity at all, you will NEVER make it in this business. This is why companies or facilities hire immigrants, illegals, and migrants from other countries. These people will do anything for nothing. These people live 20 in a one-bedroom apartment; they live in squalor. The basics are good enough for them, and this is why American companies like them. They don't bitch and moan, they require little, and they work their asses off.

I do not believe healthcare is right. Sorry. None of us are entitled to anything, and yet all of us feel entitled to everything. Although I believe healthcare isn't right, if one receives healthcare, they should be treated with the respect and love they would want to receive from someone else. Healthcare in the United States is and always has been a privilege. Healthcare is necessary, albeit still a privilege. Even before Europeans migrated to this continent, life was treated as a privilege. The indigenous peoples could not afford to take on burdens, those who could no longer contribute to the community, so they sent their old asses off into the woods to die. Sounds cruel, but it was necessary. We could do the very same thing today if we wanted to, so feel grateful your weak ass is being saved, not only cared for, through no cost out of your own pocket. Technically, those who can no longer care for themselves are burdens to society; they tax resources they are incapable of replenishing. We only have so much to go around. We can't afford to save every funky human who takes up space and sucks up all the air. We also can't sustainably handle 8 billion people on the planet. About half of that amount is all we need. I like what Bill Burr said in one of his stand-up performances, "We are the only species who save the weak." He was so right. Do you know how much money is spent to keep a sick person alive? I mean, a sick person who has no chance of recovery, who is dying, who does not live a quality life and never will? $9,000,000 per nursing home in my state alone.

That's $180,000 per resident. It's a waste of money and pointless to keep someone like that alive. I would never, never want to live to know I will never be the same again. Why? What's the point? Know what they do in nursing homes? Instead of euthanizing the dying (which is illegal and should NOT be), they allow the old fogies to starve to death. So, for two weeks straight, all you hear is grunting, moaning, and gurgling in the same room as your grandfather. He must go to bed at night, not at peace at all, and hear his roommate die. This is completely legal, yet euthanasia isn't. This country makes no sense to me whatsoever. What is up with your obsession with living so long? I don't get it. Most of the elderly suffer. Why prolong that?

Back to how to treat those you care for: Many modern nurses today are what that old, bitch nurse I spoke about called "Paper Pushers." The nurses today do not do the work of both nurses and CNAs like they used to do. According to this old nurse, these modern nurses today are lazy. They get mad when a patient asks for not one, not two, but three whole cups of juice, one after the other. In other words, these modern nurses do not want to have to go back and forth to give a patient juice. Too much work, I guess. Meanwhile, CNAs are busy wiping diarrhea ass. Imagine if the CNA said the same thing about wiping ass every day. These patients and residents would get sicker and die. In a way, it's a privilege to be a nurse. Since, compared to yesteryear, you have it easy today. I always say if you don't like your job, QUIT. Clean toilets for a living. Janitors make good, working-class money. Go for it. This old bitch nurse was a mean, old broad. She made a crass comment when a classmate of mine complimented me on how beautiful I was to her. This raggy, old cunt said, and I quote, "Don't encourage her." This old nurse was mad I wasn't crying my eyes out, like the other students, when she shared a story about an AIDS patient. Just because you are overemotional doesn't mean I should be. I thought telling that story was inappropriate, and she should have focused on the material. You still can be a kind person, and refrain from exploding into tears in public. Learn to regulate your emotions, ladies. (I see why men cheat on females like her. Females like her deserve to be treated horribly by men). So, only the sick and dying receive respect? Without people like me, the sick and dying would not receive care. You're welcome. All I did was sit there quietly, listening to the lessons. After I passed my class, some students of hers complained about her. This old broad was shocked. Wow, no idea why they tattled, huh? I talk about women and how lousy of human beings they are to others later in this narrative. Although these modern nurses are spoiled, I still feel working in healthcare is majorly tough. We do not get enough credit for the jobs that we do, and we should be the ones treated like royalty.

The Mentally Retarded

When I moved on to working for the developmentally disabled, I saw much worse. Or perhaps it was just the same; however, I could not stomach such barbaric conditions. The developmentally disabled, formally known as "Mentally Retarded," ranged from low functioning to high functioning. The high-functioning ones were way easier to handle. Not only were the high-functioning clients easier to handle, but you would also make slightly more money dealing with them. This made no sense to me whatsoever. However, the low-functioning ones were horrible to deal with on a day-to-day basis. Like I said, this business is not for the faint of heart. Some of us hate taking care of people. That's part of why I didn't have kids; I did not want to be burdened. Don't worry, I wound up being a mother anyway to the world. Anyway, we also had a range of clients who had different medical issues and backgrounds. Some, believe it or not, were pedophiles. Yep, creepy child diddlers. Yet, these freaks were allowed out in public. I am sorry, I do not agree with inclusion. Not everyone is equal; that is a fact, and not everyone can function in a normal society. Some of our clients had uncontrollable behaviors. Some are violent, and they will kick your ass. Yet, if we fight back the natural, human way, we lose our jobs. Check out my book, "The Rat," by Mary Bell, where I talk about PMT. Like I said, we can't save everyone because they can harm the rest of us. The average IQ for those with Down Syndrome is only 50. That's like having the mind of an eight-year-old for life. Do you think that you would live a quality of life with the mind of an eight-year-old while you're 40? Do you think you would be having children, getting married, working on machinery, or even working full time on anything that all requires at least an average IQ (a score of 100)? Take that low IQ and combine it with some behavioral problems. How do you think others would feel living among you? This is why we can test for Down Syndrome during pregnancy. It gives the parents an opportunity to decide about abortion. Why would you risk giving birth to someone who has an IQ of 50? You would endanger the lives of everyone surrounding you.

Don't get me started on the mentally ill. I have had crimes committed against me by the mentally ill, and they got away with it. The mentally ill get to have the freedom to refuse medication when they need it. That is unfair to the rest of us. These people are not royalty; why are we treating them as such? If people need treatment, and if they refuse it, then they don't belong with the rest of us. They belong in their little world, away from normalcy or locked up. I have had a mentally ill person, off their meds, follow me all the way home. The cops, who were saints to me, asked me if I wanted them to arrest him. Like a dumb ass, I said, "No." I regret that because if he was in jail, his family might have taken legal control and forced him on his meds. It's a shame things have to go that far in order for people to be safe. Another mentally ill person, a neighbor, yelled, screamed, and slammed doors all night long. She refused treatment. In this blue state, there was nothing the cops could do unless she did much worse. Why wait until a crime occurs before something gets done? These dummy laws are outrageous. This whacko woke up the entire building. We all must work every day and pay taxes to pay for her social security disability, so she has the luxury of being crazy all night.

Another crazy Down Syndrome person harassed me constantly, and he is mentioned in my book, "The Rat." This retard belonged behind bars, and he wasn't because the deformed organisms of the world get to do whatever they want, no matter who is hurt in the process. One client we had was tied down by his parents to the toilet because he had this issue with using the toilet (By the way, I refused to take care of him). This sounds cruel for his parents to do this, but I understand why they did this. He was uncontrollable every time he sat down on the john. To this day, healthcare workers must tolerate this nonsense. He was not abused at all; he was born like this. It was very weird. No one knows why he did not want to use the toilet. In addition to that, why on earth can't we shave his pubes? Shit would get caught in the hair. Why in the world do we have to tolerate such barbaric conditions? His life literally has no meaning and no purpose. He is suffering, and so are we. Contrary to popular belief, some Down Syndrome people have evil souls. Just like normal people vary, so do the deformed. Some of the activists of the past made my life a living hell for today.

I get criticized a lot for supporting Eugenics. Whenever I mention it, I get called 'Hitler.' The entire idea behind Eugenics, if you look up the definition, is to prevent genetic deformities from being passed on to innocent lives. Why would you want to bring someone into the world who will suffer? I am not the sick one. You people are sick to be forcing others to live, knowing they will suffer and knowing the rest of us will suffer. Furthermore, just because you can have kids, it does not mean you SHOULD. We all know there are some shitty parents out there. I mean, come on, people. We have parents who severely abuse their kids, and you want them to breed? We can kind of guess who would have the potential to harm others and who is so messed up they will pass on bad genes to others. So, why not sterilize them? Again, you want people to suffer. Then, my suggestion is you take care of every fucking person who is sick, traumatized, violent, commits crimes, etc. I recommend you pay for their care, their shelter, their therapy, their food, their clothing, their education, etc. How many people do you think exist who do nothing but harm society? You want these fuckers alive so badly you are willing to risk more people being raped or murdered. I am not suggesting we sterilize people based on stupid reasons like race or religion. I am suggesting we sterilize people who have bad genetics, which they can pass down, and who are incapable of raising the next generation properly.

A lot of folks are ill-equipped for child-rearing. We're not always going to get our way. In fact, we will experience a lot of disappointments. Something must be sacrificed. What are you willing to sacrifice to gain? What are you willing to give up for the greater good? You're not in this world alone. Others are surrounding you who must put up with you. The kind, generous thing to do is to be a bit more reasonable and do what is best for ALL, not just for you. This is the problem with the USA, it's always about individuals and not the group, who must tolerate these individuals. What about the poor? If you can't afford children, you should not have them. Point blank. Children out of poverty will more than likely remain in poverty. Poverty comes with a lot of problems: poor health, poor education, crime, abuse, etc. How is that a good thing? I remember some old Libby – white cunt called my WW2 vet grandfather a "waste." It took everything in my power not to stab her to death (I had my grandfather's knife with me, too, at the time). I should have called her disabled granddaughter "a waste" also, as she was sitting in her wheelchair right by us. The fact is my grandfather was useful to society and made sacrifices, and her granddaughter's life could have been prevented because we have no use for her.

Ramblings Continued...

It's unfair for an innocent child to be brought up in poverty when they will most likely remain in poverty. I read that people tend to have more kids when they experience a scarcity of resources. It's the Human Primate that panics and says, "We're starving, and we need more people to help keep our species going!" Conversely, people who are plentiful with their resources have fewer children. They want to conserve what they have for fear of losing. Right now, in industrialized nations, the birth rate is low, and in poor, starving nations, they are creating more primates. Proves the science of this. That TikTok chick who argued with me about Eugenics said we should give people a chance and educate them. Look, we have said a lot of things to a lot of people, and people do not listen. They're gonna behave like monkeys anyway. I find the best way to change human behavior is through consequences. When you want a certain behavior changed, you offer an outcome to that behavior that is unpleasant. A primate will associate that behavior with that particular outcome, and then that undesired behavior becomes extinct. It's called "Extinction" in Psychology. We can encourage the desired behavior by offering a pleasant outcome to that behavior. For instance, from what I heard, California drug-addicted mothers were offered 40K if they agreed to sterilization. They took the offer, of course. Now, that's encouraging the desired behavior. I agree with what California did here. Why would you want drug-addicted, mentally ill women to be pregnant? You people are sick if you think that is okay. My only critique is that they should sterilize the men, too. Male sterilization is easier, simpler, and probably cheaper. If you're uneducated and dumb, you shouldn't have kids. This is an obvious one. You would not raise the kids properly; not knowing about the proper way to treat, teach, and rear a child will lead to that child being fucked up. Again, you are creating more stupid people to exist in this world.

Nothing positive comes out of poverty. You could argue that the ability to overcome and develop resiliency is a positive. I will say, "Yeah, but at what cost?" I've seen nothing but bad behaviors come from poor neighborhoods. Nothing I've witnessed was good. These people should not create more of them. These female liberal activists were the ones responsible for giving the worst humans on the planet freedom or second chances. Women are ridiculous, and they are partly to blame for the violent men they complain about. If you present severe consequences to really bad behavior, that will discourage people from exhibiting that behavior. We used to do that until women participated in the "Let's treat evil beings like saints" movement. Giving people a pat on the back, a leg up, and second chances will only keep those criminals you complain about alive. Women sabotage themselves because of their unnecessary, dramatic feelings without realizing how their feelings affect the rest of us. Women also give birth to these crappy primates and take no responsibility for it. She is so "strong and independent" yet so unwilling to take responsibility for her actions. Strong women own up to their mistakes. Speaking of women…read on.

I Am A Woman, Hear Me Purr?

I happened to be a college dropout. I've made more working a 9-5 job than my white male counterparts, who have college degrees. As a biracial woman, how was I able to do this? I will tell you one thing: my race nor my gender ever got in the way of my ability to acquire success. We hear an awful lot about black women, or women in general, making so much less than men, especially white men. I will tell you one reason, one major reason, some women make less than men: CHILDREN, that's the reason. It's common sense that having children, in general, is a major interruption in our lives. Children take time, energy, and money away from us. Knowing that the primary caregivers of children are most likely women, it makes sense that some women would make less than their male counterparts. (Male/Female Earnings Differences in Self-Employment: The Effects of Marriage, Children, and the Household Division of Labor - Greg Hundley, 2000 (sagepub.com). Women are more than likely to bear the brunt of childcare & household chores, which leave little room for career advancement. Case in point, in a high school in my area, a predominantly black high school, young teenage girls were getting pregnant on purpose just to get time from school and collect welfare, according to a New London High School teacher. Now, how are women earning less due to discrimination if they are CHOOSING to break that career path by having children? Apparently, according to Instagram, in the year 2030, about 45% of women will be foregoing motherhood, and thank goodness they will be choosing to be free instead of burdening their lives with brats. I mean, conservatives should be happy. These liberals won't be breeding. Fewer Kamala supporters on the planet.

Despite this pretend wage gap nonsense, women happen to be more formally educated, and nowadays, more women are waiting until they are older to have kids (The Long-Term Decline in

Fertility—and What It Means for State Budgets | The Pew Charitable Trusts (pewtrusts.org)). How on Earth is the gender wage gap due to discrimination? It's not. It's due to the fact that some female parents are out of the working world for long periods of time, they take much time off work, they leave early, they arrive late, and they don't put in the time to pursue an education to further their careers. Their careers are their children. I hated working alongside single mothers. I did their work for them, and I thought I should have been given their paycheck. Why should someone in that scenario make as much as someone who has put in time, effort, and money into their job? That's unfair. That's unjust, and I don't call that equality. I call that giving baby mamas special treatment, which is what women really want, special treatment. So, you know how to lie on your back, spread your legs open, and get fucked like a whore. Congratulations. You don't get a reward for that. It was your choice. You could have chosen differently. 80% of women who get pregnant choose babies, and you have the option to choose differently. Don't get me started on this child tax credit bullshit. Really? Getting free money for doing what gorillas do (I don't feel anyone should get tax credits, and this is the one thing I disagree with Trump about giving breeders free money. How do you know their kids will turn out great?) Women are making great money and, at times, surpassing men. Hey, I'm here for it. You do you, girl! However, for those who choose children, choose wisely. I'm certainly not gonna pick up the slack at work because of your maternity leave. I want to get paid to be home too. I don't call that equality. That's giving human incubators SPECIAL treatment.

In addition to taking time off work due to kids, women are often very passive in the working world. These so-called "strong and independent" women rarely advocate for themselves in the workplace. If you want a higher salary, dummy, ASK for it. If you think for a second that your employers are kind, empathetic entities who will give you more money out of the kindness of their hearts, you have another thing coming. You must do what men do; you have to HUNT. Women's lack of aggressiveness in the working world is another reason why there is a gender wage gap. Sure. Are there some stigmas out there about women? Of course, but I do not think those stigmas are the major reasons why women are making less.

It is unfair for a company and for other employees to accommodate working parents. We should not flip the bill to pay for your daycare, nor should we take on the extra work because you have had a baby when you COULD HAVE CHOOSEN DIFFERENTLY. I did not force you to have a kid. That was YOUR choice. I have no guarantee that your child will be a great member of society. In addition to that, according to research, stay-at-home moms are happier than working moms. Why? Because stay at home moms are not burning the candle on both ends. Imagine being so stupid into thinking you can do everything like a superhero just because you have a vagina. Choose a path, dummy. If you are not gonna fight like men, then you will NOT have the pay like men. It's that simple. Let me tell you something very interesting: I read a comment on Instagram from someone about gender differences. Now, I did check to see if this person was right, and yes, he was right. Here is his comment:

Comments

interactions, while boys are more likely to play with toys that involve mechanical functions or actions.

One notable study that supports this idea is the research linked to the Gender Equality Paradox, particularly evident in countries like Norway. The paradox reveals that in societies with higher gender equality, occupational gender differences become more pronounced. This has been extensively discussed in studies by Richard A. Lippa and others who analyzed patterns of interest across cultures. For example, Lippa's 2010 study "Gender Differences in Personality and Interests: When, Where, and Why?" highlights these trends.

Reply

gabrielmarksmith 19h

Someone conditioned you to open

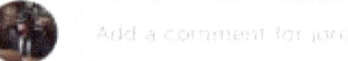

Add a comment for jordanpetersononc

He was trying to convey that when you push gender equality, as in pushing men and women into the opposite from the more traditional gender-occupational roles, this makes men and women revert even more back to their original gender roles. In other words, if you were to push women to be more interested in things, they would eventually develop an aversion to that and go back to being interested in people. So, although there are more women entering tech and physical science fields, this will not take off, as it has been tried before. Women, collectively, will wind up going back to social science fields or fields associated with "helping people" and/or office work, etc. Here is the link to the study this guy was referencing: Microsoft Word - Master thesis_kaja.docx The Norwegian Labour Market, a Gender Equality Paradox? A Qualitative Case Study of Norway from the 1970s until today Kaja Eriksrød UNIVERSITY OF BERGEN Department of Comparative Politics Master thesis Spring 2021.

We all know that Norway, Sweden, and Swiss research is way more objective and accurate than our current, politicized American research. These areas of the world are thought of as being more "progressive" than the United States by hippy libbies. Ironically, these areas' research findings almost always disprove these libbies theories. What women should focus on is EQUITY, not EQUALITY. There are some female leaders out there, but women tend to lack the natural skills men have to lead. Men are more decisive on the job. They have a 'take charge' attitude and make decisions quickly. Men are better at developing strategies for solving problems. Women tend to be micro-managers (I have had female bosses, so I know this to be true). Micromanaging is an ineffective way to accomplish goals, and it leads to resentment as well as lowered work morale. In addition, men are direct in their communication. Women, not so much. So, yeah, women can be leaders, but are they effective leaders? Yeah, women can participate in male-dominated fields, but do we have to lower our standards just to allow women in the mix? From what I hear, this happens. I heard that in many fields (like the military and the fire department), standards are lowered so that women can enter these challenging occupations. I understand why men are pissed if this is the case. I don't know about you, but I want someone qualified to fly a plane when I travel to Florida. I am not interested in dying prematurely.

The feminists will say that what deters women from these male fields is sexual harassment. I say that's not true. Most women aren't interested in these jobs, to begin with, and you can still experience sexual harassment in gender-neutral occupations, with even women as the culprits. However, I can tell you that to be equal to a man, you have to fight like one. So, if MOST women, that's 80% of the American female population, go into these male-dominated fields, you can push the men out. If MOST women stuck together as a team-cause we all know most women make horrible team players as a collective, we can fairly compete with our male counterparts. As it stands now, women just aren't wired to be drawn to plumbing, construction, or engineering. We all know about those rare cases of women, yes, and women have made some great strides lately, but let's see how many women enter these male fields over time. Pay attention to the next 30 years, and let's see what happens. As it stands now, women in these fields are a minority, and men heavily dominate these fields.

So, ladies, if you want change, if you truly want equality, you're gonna have to start to act like a man. A man who has the personality type of a trucker or an oil rigger. You must behave exactly how these men behave, and you must learn how to compete with them. Men compete with other men, too, so you're not alone. This is exactly what equality means, ladies. EQUITY, on the other hand means to have fairness within your respective roles. EQUITY is when both genders are treated fairly based on their own unique abilities. There are some significant biological differences between men and women; why are you trying to fight against that so much? Of course, you do have the option of transitioning into a man if you want to try to be equal to one. Go for it, suga. I've heard trans-men complaining a lot about feeling "cut off" from their emotions after transitioning. So, have fun with that.

Back to the entitled, American mother: I remember a time when this mother's son was running around like a maniac. He stepped on my foot and knocked this elderly woman over, and this mother's response was, "My son has special needs!" So? It's your responsibility to learn how to be a good mother. It's your responsibility to learn how to manage special needs children. The rest of us should not have to be inconvenienced by your kid or your choice to have kids. The world does not revolve around you, sweetie. Don't have kids if you can't handle raising them. I told the grandparents, who were sitting at the table, "You are the grandparents; you should know better."

Sorry to say, ladies, you cannot and will not have it all. You will never be a perfect mother, career woman, and wife, all at the same time. Something will be sacrificed. You choose a life that resonates with your soul the most. For some, it's baby-making; for others, it's work. Choose a path. You cannot properly be a good mother working full-time. I disagree with people here. Realistically and practically, when you're at work, other people are watching your kids. So, it is impossible to be everywhere all the time, right? However, if you are going to be a mother, I think women should choose to stay home or just stick to part-time work. Or marry a rich man so he can afford to take care of you and the kids, or get rich yourself and relax at home so you have time to be a good mother to your children. The early years of a human's life are uber important, and the time spent during these early years should be with the mother. Working during these critical moments with your offspring will fuck it up, no doubt. No matter what, you should be planning for children and marriage, and we all know women never plan when they have relationships with men. They often fantasize about the wedding and the cute baby and NEVER think about the actual reality of the work involved in both marriage and children. You are no superhero, and you never will be. You are human, by definition, being human means you are vulnerable as well as imperfect. You are very much penetrable, just like any man. You will naturally fail as a mother when you choose work over your kids. You will naturally take out your stressed-out day onto your kids, and kids are sensitive, so they will be negatively affected by your angry, aggressive attitude. As a mother, you're supposed to be kind, loving, and nurturing, not angry.

I looked up the stats about women who work and the husband who stays at home. You know what I found out? The divorce rates are higher for career women than for women who choose to focus on being a mother (By the way, the divorce rates are the lowest with couples who are religiously inclined). Even in the presence of no children, househusbands have issues with staying at home, and it's not because of their male egos, as women claim, but because what comes along with a career woman is a bad attitude, disrespect, domineering behavior, aggression, anger, and emasculation. I am not being biased here; I am giving facts. It takes work to set your feelings aside to find the most accurate truth that exists. It especially takes work sifting through this politicized American science. I want to know the entire situation, not just something that makes me feel better. It's funny; I saw a vid on Instagram by a popular creator who makes a living shitting on men instead of coming up with solutions to end this gender war. Here is a snapshot of her video...

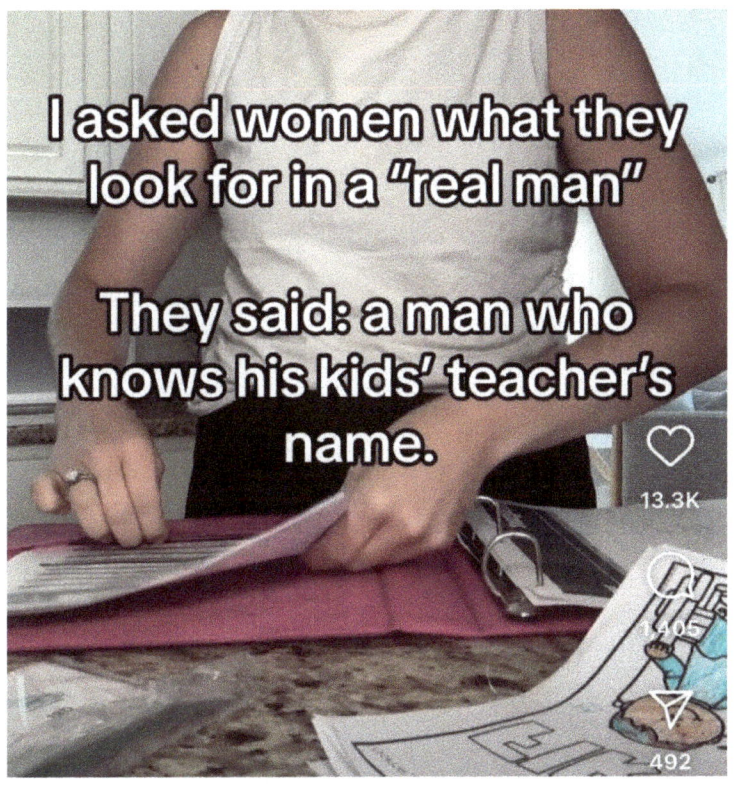

So, I bring this up because working moms often complain that their husbands do not share the household chores or domestic labor. When I talk to men to get their perspective, I hear a lot of men break down the activities they participate in at home, but they add this important fact: Women see things differently from men. So, in the man's view he is contributing 50%, but according to the woman, he is barely doing anything. What takes women 6 hours to complete at home, men can do it within 2.5 hours. The reason why it takes men a shorter time to complete tasks is that men do not fuss over minuscule details that really don't matter. The trash doesn't need to be taken out immediately when you say so. You do not need to wash the dishes BEFORE placing them into the dishwasher. No need to add 20,000 decorative pillows to a bed; two are all you need. You do not need to deep-clean the house every single day; clean up as you go. You don't need to plan a birthday party for a 4-year-old, so the plethora of tasks on your list is unnecessary. Buy one thing, you're done. Kids remember love more than presents or parties. We all grew up riding bicycles without helmets and knee pads; he did not forget your son's helmet; he just thought it was unnecessary. Women create more work for themselves than necessary, and men focus on what is necessary. What gets the job done, not how it is done. Get it? So, in the case of this video, there is no need to know a teacher's name, especially since teachers change with every passing grade. At 45, I do not remember ANY of my teachers' names, and I couldn't care less if my mom cared to know their names either. I care about the major stuff, and your kids will, too. What you should be more worried about is how your child is doing in school. Good, bad? Ok, great. Any major issues? No? Ok, move on then. Teachers don't remember every kid and every parent's name either. Is your child happy about life? That is more important than the teacher's name. No need to kill yourself over every little, tiny aspect of life. Men kind of sum shit up in one shot and focus on the end goal. There are a million other important, major things men worry about. Something like a chronic health issue is way more important than a teacher's name. Men cannot fit all this info in their brains, they focus on the important stuff. Men are busy driving kids to their activities, to and from appointments, to and from school, helping with homework, working fulltime, helping in the house, just not to YOUR liking. So, my take is it's not that men do not contribute to this stuff, it's just that women aren't satisfied with the way or how men do things.

There is no such thing as weaponized incompetence. Men are exhausted hearing women bitch and moan over nonsense; the men just give up and say, "Fine, you do it then since I don't do anything right according to you." Then, women wonder why men cheat. He doesn't act like a child; you TREAT him like one. Your way isn't necessarily the best way to do something, and it certainly isn't the only way. Often, women think they know everything, and the way they do things is right, perfect, and the end all be all, without regarding how maybe men have something to offer, maybe men are right about some things. Let him take over, complete a task on his own, his way, without your butting in telling him he's wrong. You want a masculine man, a leader, but you're unwilling to allow him to take over doing the laundry. LOL. Make that make sense. I do not fold some of my clothes either. It's unnecessary. Some things do not need to be hung up. Relax. It ain't that serious. It's a towel. So, he folded it the way you don't like it; at least it is folded. You wonder why relationships fall apart. Maybe kids need a "relationship" class taken in high school. Some sort of life class that teaches everything you need to know and learn in preparation for adult life. It appears parents aren't raising children properly if, when these kids become men and women, they struggle with keeping their relationships together.

Here are some testimonies coming from men I found on Instagram: By the way, I asked Gemini, the AI robot, about men's research, and Gemini told me, in her condescending female voice, that there isn't enough research currently reporting the perspectives nor the feelings of men. I can tell there isn't because when I try to look up surveys about how MEN FEEL, I can never find much of anything. In this female-dominated political climate, the focus is on women, and the focus should be on BOTH GENDERS, their thoughts, their perceptions, their feelings, their wants, and their needs, not just women.

Comments

View 23 more replies

therefore69 11w
Because they don't like the way men do housework. My wife used to complain I didn't help with housework so I did, she nitpicked and complained about the way I did everything (wasn't 100% the way she did it) so I told we her If I am going to get ragged on for not helping and I'm going to get ragged on for helping...guess which one I choose. I haven't done any housework in 30 years.
9

Reply

View 7 more replies

essieelleneffy 2d
Many men r dependent on women to act as
their mommies

 Add a comment for shelsapaige

26

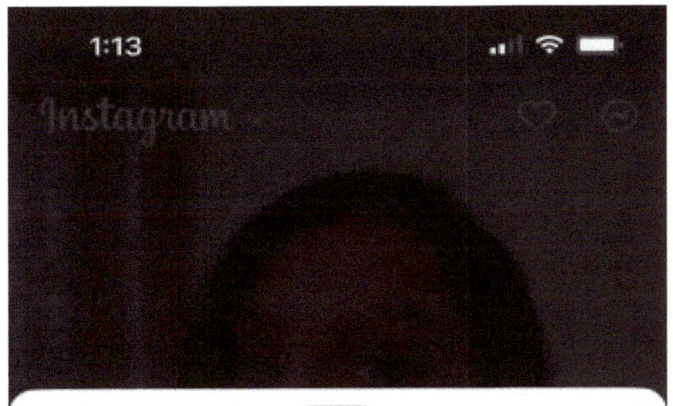

Comments

So the fact that he was gone before you got up, and came home after you had everything done obviously holds no bearing. He's out fighting dragons and monsters to give you the life you have, the home you have and the ability to get up with kids. He doesn't bring his problems homes because he doesn't want to burden you or doesn't want to hear how it makes you feel. Should he do more to help yes, but he probably doesn't because he got tired of being told he's doing it wrong and watching you do it over your way. He probably doesn't say much to you because it always ends up in a fight and he wants to avoid that.

Him wanting to have physical relations with you isn't about the physical, it's because he loves you, finds you attractive and it's the best way he knows how to express being close to you. You telling him no is him being rejected by you, and he takes that as you don't desire him, and ultimately

13

 Add a comment for caylaecresta

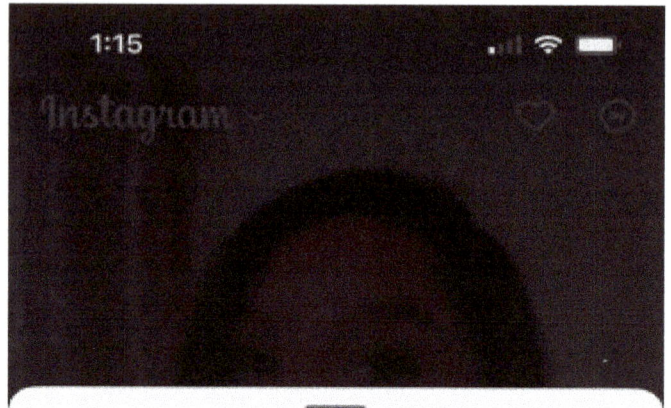

Comments

that they also provide the stability for the family, the safety and security factor. Married men will sacrifice their happiness for the happiness of the family. Nobody ask dad if he's happy, or generally how he's doing. Men don't generally talk about their feelings because they don't feel safe doing it, even with their wives. The house is the wife's, even the husbands acknowledges this. Go through a house and find a room that belongs to the man, one he decorated and can call his own. You won't because they don't exist. Now, again I believe a man is responsible to take care of the house as well, and not just the outside. But if you want it done don't tell him he did it wrong just because he did it differently from you. You want it done your way do it yourself. You want him involved doing things around the house be thankful when he is doing things not upset he

 Add a comment for cayleecresta

So, ladies, you see here that what men are looking for are the exact qualities you ladies CLAIM you possess. Being loving, listening, caring, being kind, generous, having EMPATHY for your man or men in general, etc. Women are NOT the experts of empathy if they REFUSE to take a man's feelings into consideration. If you claim that you are the master of empathy, then that means you have empathy FOR ALL HUMANS IN ALL SITUATIONS (Empathy: Gender effects in brain and behavior - PMC-National Library of Medicine). So, because men often abuse women, they also have a hard time separating the bad experiences or the bad men from the good ones. They often place ALL men in the same category. I am not denying all the realities about men and their biological nature; however, I also am a rational person who can put aside feelings and look at life exactly as it is, as objectively as possible, without my personal biases. This is hard for people to do, in general, but especially hard for hurt women WHO HAVE NOT HEALED from their pain from men. You know you are past the hurt when you look at people as all having the same thing in common, no matter their race, gender, socio-economic status, etc. All humans are connected by the very same things we all need to survive. Not just our need for food, water, or shelter but also our need to feel valued, loved, important, etc. These men were being vulnerable in these comments, and not ONE woman expressed any form of empathy for them. Their comments were ignored and unrecognized. Women's struggles should not take away from the struggles of men. Yes, women are important, no doubt, there are a lot of things men need to do as a collective and as individuals, absolutely. However, even without men in the picture, women are still imperfect beings who also have a lot to learn and who must improve not only as a collective but also as individuals.

The study from above said that in certain situations, women are very critical of women more so than they are critical of men, naturally. Why do you think women like me prefer a man's company so much? Women, who are often found as a threat to other women, are treated horribly by those women who feel threatened. We are not "pick me;" we go where we are loved, valued, and appreciated. Why should I pick a woman who treats me like shit just because I exist? Pretty privilege isn't a thing when you are hated and treated poorly by an entire gender. Instead of being jealous of other women, why don't you improve yourself? Instead of being jealous of other women, why don't you admire them? Some women are, in fact, better than you. Deal with it, and work hard to be just as good as them, or accept your shitty self the way you are. I have never in my life been jealous of other women to only then seek out to destroy them. In fact, when I see an attractive woman, a woman who looks way better than I do, I stay humble. I admire her. I compliment her. I say to myself, "Wow, she looks good. I should work out so my butt can look like that." I take the opportunity to not only show that women support me but also evaluate how I could do better. That is the healthiest way to respond to other women whom you feel are better than you in some way. If your immediate reaction is to insult her, critique her, or say something negative, sweetheart, you are in some serious pain within yourself. You need more than a therapist. You need an exorcism. Women tend to have power in human social interactions. These interpersonal relationships are necessary for our survival, and if a woman hates you because you are prettier, you can lose any social capital you need to survive. Without functioning relationships with other humans, we die. This is why we need men. If you destroy another woman's life because you're jealous, a man should step in to put you in your place and resolve the conflict. Your inadequacies have nothing to do with me. If you feel "less than" around me, then maybe you should take that opportunity to make yourself better. So, many times, women lack empathy. Women are very imperfect, naturally, just like men, regardless of men's existence.

People often blame this idea of the patriarchy as to why some women are messed up, as if men are the only reason why any woman in the world does something bad. If men did not exist, apparently, women would be perfect beings, never doing anything wrong, and this world would be perfect. It will be a paradise with no negativity whatsoever. Well, none of us know a world without men, so you cannot predict how life would be without men. I can say this, though, that there are aspects of women that exist that come with being a woman that have absolutely nothing to do with men. These aspects are not always helpful, needed, or appropriate for every situation in life. A great example is the one I gave up above about women focusing on details. There are times when being detail-orientated is helpful and hurtful. It depends. I couldn't care less if you call this a stereotype. I disagree with you. (Stereotypes come from somewhere, actual events, or observed behaviors. They just don't fall from the sky onto our laps). These are qualities that are not necessarily productive in many situations. When you need things resolved quickly, and there is no time to think over anything, you need to focus on the situation at hand and come up with a solution. What is important at that particular moment? Women are just as competitive as men, but they are competitive with different things. Women LOVE drama, arguing, gossiping, going on and on and on about nothing, going off-topic, draining everyone's energy with their incessant complaining, chatter, always having an issue with life, people, places, things, being uptight, never learning how to take a joke-especially at their own expense, being bitchy, catty, rude, arrogant, all to higher degrees than men. I see women fight each other way more than men fight each other online in comment sections of these social media apps. Sure, the occasional "at a girl," but mostly, arguing about who is a better mother, who looks better, etc. Women always feel they are always right and NEVER wrong. Sure, the modern feminists claim she is pro-women until another woman challenges her ideals, her thoughts, and her feelings, disagrees with her about something, or even presents the RIGHT research to support claims made. The modern woman is pro-woman until another woman holds her accountable for mistakes. The modern woman is a pro-woman until she runs into a woman who is better looking and who receives a lot of attention from men. I thought you were pro-woman, and peace and love and all this hippy dippy love, man? What happened? You're only pro-woman when the woman is a Kamala supporter, huh? I get it now. You pick and choose whom you have empathy for or who deserves respect. If that is the case, it sounds like you aren't perfect after all. Sounds like this is an example of how the patriarchy isn't to blame for your lack of acceptance of other women who disagree with you.

Even in a world without men, guess what would happen? Women would feel MORE CONFIDENT being OVERTLY nasty, aggressive, and violent towards each other. Why? Because there are NO MEN around to subdue women. With men around, women have learned to be docile, probably for safety reasons (although, nowadays, I see more women becoming just as aggressive as men). Imagine if you take men out of the equation. Women would fear less as they would be around their equals. They would feel more confident in a conflict with other women, holding their own, standing their ground, and becoming braver and braver. Eventually, violence will resurface in the environment, and you will have, once again, DIVERSITY. Just visit any female prison, ask any CO at a female prison, or a nurse at a female prison, and you will see what I'm talking about. Women ARE NOT the gentler sex. Not at all. Later in this narrative, you will see I am right. Women seem to forget they are PRIMATES. Humans are a type of APE, and what comes along with that are certain APELIKE characteristics. You forget, as a woman, you are still as emotional and volatile as any man. Having a nasty, smelly pussy doesn't make you some holier-than-thou super goddess. It makes you a primate. A primate who has hairy, onion-smelling armpits, mud butt with toilet paper stuck to it, bloody copper-smelling period, egg-stank farts-these are all primate realities, not divinity. Slow ya roll, girly.

Back to the working woman: Contrary to popular belief, husbands, on average, work longer hours per week than wives. It's only fair the one who works less outside of the home does more inside of the home. That's called equality, ladies. While you ladies are worried about husbands remembering teachers' names, arguing with your husbands, and fussing over washing the dishes before they are placed into the dishwasher, your 14-year-old daughter is being groomed by a pedophile on TikTok. Your son is inhaling laughing gas and watching scat porn. The amount of young people I see in comments on TikTok and Instagram without being supervised by an adult is crazy to me. The fact that children are allowed on social media to begin with is even crazier. Great mothering ladies (rolling my eyes). All this stuff about what to expect when married with children should be discussed and found out before marriage and kids. How do you two operate living together? What are your goals with children, etc? Women often do not think about these things because, once again, they live in la la land and romanticize the wedding without grounding their energy and thinking about the actual marriage.

It is impossible to be the mother and the father at the same time. Sons and daughters need their daddies. As long as men exist, fathers are needed. Face it; you ladies aren't goddesses, nor are you Mary, the mother of Jesus. The more you treat your daughters like they're little princesses, incapable of doing wrong, the more women will feel entitled once these women become partners with other men. Let that sink in. Re-read the previous sentence again. The latest trend is women decentering the men in their lives. I challenge you "strong and independent" women to go a few steps further and decenter your sons, fathers, brothers, and so on. They can be just as toxic as your boyfriends and husbands, and remember; they are also boyfriends and husbands to other women. Some of your fathers were assholes, as well as your brothers, but you give them a break. Do you want men to change? Raise them right in the first place. Raise your sons better. Teach your sons how to be good partners for women. Raise your boys the way you want men to be in this world. Or stop giving birth to boys if life is that bad with men around. The same goes for dads and their daughters. Raise your daughters how you want women to be. Be the change and the solution, people, not the problem. You girls gave birth to these boys and raised them improperly. Now, you gotta deal with the consequences. You should have done what I've done-swallowed. *Slurp*

This brings me to the other reason why some women make less than men or even other women. Some women, other than wasting their time having kids, waste their time on lousy, low-paying jobs that happen to be female-dominated jobs. Men make a lot because the men do the jobs that most women aren't interested in doing. God forbid we should break a nail, right ladies? There are some dangerous, tough jobs out there that men do; men are naturally risk-takers (Daring Differently: Gender Differences in Risk-Taking Behavior - Neuroscience News), so it's easy for them to manage the extremely unpleasant tasks some of their jobs entail that women curl their noses towards. They tend to be passive and lack the courage it takes to climb that corporate ladder. Or, at other times, a real ladder. Although some women are climbing that ladder more and more, most are still not interested in becoming leaders. They take the road of the follower. Women cannot even get along with each other longer than a minute, and you think men are the problem? You have women on this planet who also disagree with you. Look at the women who voted for Trump vs. women who voted for Kamala. Imagine a world with no men. My lord, the amount of arguing that would take place would be insurmountable. The bickering, the backstabbing, the manipulation, the lies, the cheating, the jealousy, most of all! Women would be competing about who is the better mother. I can see it already. Men balance us out and vice versa. With or without the patriarchy, there's no excuse for being a bitch, especially to other women. Even in a matriarchal society, you broads would still give the worst humans, who need to die, second chances. If you want the type of change you Libby ladies are looking for, you must get ALL women on your side. As it stands now, girly, you have some competition. Good luck with that.

Women want change, but they are unwilling to get along and stick together. Welp, deal with men, then. One thing a man is great at is being a good team player. Women, not so much. Female sports would be more popular if women supported other women. I, myself love watching female MMA fighters. I happen to love sports, and I support female athletes. In reality, catty shows are more interesting to females. You were brainwashed as a child into thinking you're a princess who is incapable of wrongdoing. Then, you go out into the world as adults and see just how much Disney lied to you. You romanticize everything without seeing reality for what it is or accepting that reality. You bad mothers are making decent women look bad. I 100% hold you accountable. Women make up half the world, and they are half responsible for the problems in this world. Remember that. Some stupid broad asked me on TikTok, "What have women done that was life-altering in a negative way?" In other words, she meant men are the only ones who destroy lives. I responded, "Women do plenty; they become bad mothers." John Wayne Gacy, Ted Bundy, and Jeffery Dahmer all had mothers. What were those bitches like? Saints? Goddesses? I think not! In fact, Ted Bundy's mother made excuses for her son's killings, calling him, and I quote, "a good boy." She should have said, "Execute that bastard, judge." I rest my case.

Another thing this TikTok, ditzy broad, did was make excuses for women's bad behavior. "Oh, they were abused, la la da da a etc." Look, if you want me to have compassion for women, it's only fair that we extend that same compassion to men. Equality, right? So, if a man hurts a woman, oh, I feel so sorry for him. He was abused as a child. That's why he abuses now. See how pathetic that sounds, although there might be some truth to it. It's okay to hate men, but not okay to hate women, who equally hurt others in many ways. No matter how badly you were hurt, you are still responsible for your behavior and your healing. Men get hurt, too. Where is their compassion? They get hurt, but they still are supposed to be held accountable. They get hurt, but they are expected to suck it up. Why can't you, females, suck it up? You can't measure pain and say yours was worse than mine. Pain is subjective. I will EQUALLY hold you responsible for your bad behaviors and bad choices. Men are not the only guilty ones here. Do you want equality? Okay, go shovel shit, pave roads, build bridges, farm, and any other job that is male-dominated. Not gonna? Most of you are not interested in those jobs, you say? You're also not naturally physically stronger than a man.

Women can be very problematic. Women are so skilled at communication in a way that their words are sharp and hurt deep. Modern women only have empathy for those they can relate to. Case in point here is my response to a woman on Instagram about the pain she has from men.

@chaneedelgado2310 well you responded to a comment that gave the example of a man surprising and being decisive and YOU took it to an entirely different level about abuse which is different. A man saying "hey I got tickets for a show let's go" is the most simplest innocent kind gesture a person can display without abusing that's not abusive that is as you say " a surprise that was decisive " however you interpreted a man's thoughtfulness as something very negative which tells me you have some emotional attachment towards abuse or some pain from men that has not been addressed whether it was your sister or not that pain is still within you . Again this topic was not about abuse so there was no need for you to take it to that level . You added information that was off topic and it only prevents ghe main message from being misunderstood.

Reply

View 1 more reply

So, not only did this chick NOT stick to the topic at hand by bringing up UNRELATED information (as women do often), but she likened abuse with a man being kind to his woman. Masculinity is not a negative, and I do not know why this trend nowadays says it is. What is wrong with a powerful, strong man? Women can be strong, but men can't? I am convinced most women are just lesbians who don't even like men as people, and when you do not heal from pain, you tend not to see men as people but as ENEMIES. Everything some of these women are looking for, they will only find in a woman. Go date a woman, then. The difference between masculinity and femininity is the difference between ACTION and INACTION. That's it. Femininity is taking a back seat, and masculinity is taking charge or acting. Even the most successful career women are still women, and by nature, there are certain qualities a woman has that will never change. On average, men have better spatial reasoning than women. Angry, lesbian or not, spatially, a man will do better. It is possible that a man can show empathy and be masculine at the same time. Unfortunately, a lot of bitter women conflate abuse with masculinity. Masculinity in and of itself is normal and healthy. Masculinity is needed. Career women know this fact. This is why they are seen as masculine by men. This energy is needed to achieve goals. You need to take ACTION to see things through, and when you are hyper-focused on a career, you are saturated with masculine energy, which makes you an unappealing partner to a masculine man. Masculine, heterosexual men do not find you intimidating at all; this is a common misconception masculine women have about men (See the above picture). Men are intimidated by their equals, other men, not their opposites, women. Men do not see you as equals; this is why they don't find you to be a threat. Only women and gays see you as a threat because they see you as their equal. Men are sexually and psychologically turned off by masculine women simply because they are heterosexual, masculine men. They find you to be a turn-off, a boner shrinker if you will.

Comments

the feeling of having the upper hand somehow.

Reply

 jbennybenny 5h
I'm gonna give you some insight here no man is intimidated by you. No one is intimidated by you or anything that you have accomplished. What happened when you went into the "professional world" is that your expectations of a man went up, but your value did not go up accordingly with it that makes you irritating, not intimidating.

1

Reply

 jbennybenny 5h
Now go ahead and tell me how I'm wrong, even though I've lived numerous decades and dated

 Add a comment for therealbradle

When it comes to being a romantic partner, masculine men do not care about your career or your education. Men are capable of financially supporting themselves, and they are not interested in having you support them like they're sissies (unless you're with an effeminate dude). Men care about how you are going to treat them as people. Are you loving, respectful, nurturing, annoying, argumentative etc? Nine times out of ten, women who are career-driven tend to have off-putting personalities. They tend to be unlikeable, unkind, unempathetic, bitchy, mean, angry, jealous, vindictive, malicious, aggressive, and animalistic. Even when you consider two educated, wealthy people, male and female, who decide to marry and have kids, according to research, in that situation, 9 times out of 10, the female partner will choose to stay home. These men did not become successful by being feminine. A masculine personality is needed to be super successful. Even the successful, educated men want feminine, stay-at-home mothers. Hypervigilant career women confuse passion with anger. You aren't passionate, you're angry. There is a difference. You can be passionate and come off gently at the same time. How you are coming across is quite angry. In your delusional mind, you're normal. To the rest of the world, both men and women, you are quite hurt.

The modern women have come from a long line of women who might not have been the pioneers or visionaries of yesteryear. These women were average wives and mothers, so it seems as though the modern woman has something to prove to herself. She is rebelling against the past. Determined not to feel trapped by kids and a husband, so, she is hypervigilant when it comes to men. She has inherited pain from her mother and grandmothers, and generational trauma, unhealed, comes across as an off-putting personality in women. So, the American woman went from everything is about others but myself, to everything is about me and no one else. It is fine to make things about you until you have kids, a husband, or other relationships in your life. Then, everything cannot be about you. It's fine to make things about you until you negatively affect an entire society. The modern woman is very selfish, thinking only about herself and not how HER CHOICES affect others. Your vote for Kamala affects me. Your choice to have kids and work at the same time affects me.

When women are unhealed, they see men as the enemy. Men are people, just like you. Men can do bad and good, just like you. Men have feelings, just like you. Men have wants and desires, just like you. Men hurt, just like you. So, women tend to swing on opposite extremes. Viewing men as Prince Charming's in the beginning to evil villains towards the end. This is why women were thought to have hysteria years ago because of these mood swings. Looking at men as all good or all bad is super nuts and is a sign of a human who is super emotional and delirious. I do not consider someone who is delirious "strong and independent." Now, I see why women did not have the right to vote. I want women to vote, only if they do not vote with their feelings, but rather, based upon rationality.

Here's another broad, a therapist, apparently, who felt the need to emasculate a man online for a simple comment. That is a really innocent comment. So, I chimed in.

see. You mentioned kindness healing humility etc well your words to this man were condescending , lacked empathy (for someone you claimed is hurting) very arrogant (which is the opposite of what you suggested to him) , and delusional (his comments were just an evaluation of attractiveness coming from a male perspective) now this video he responded to was in fact displaying the same tone as you targeting men's emotions or trying to trigger men. This video is an example of a lack of humility something you accused this young man of. Part of being a therapist a professional one who attended the best schools and training who went beyond a masters as well, is having empathy for all including those who give you the "ick" your comments were as judgmental as his in addition your advice was unwarranted and unsolicited . Nobody asked for your help so why do you feel the need to give it? Myself ? I never claimed to be holier than thou but I do call out hypocrisy when I see coming from those who do claimed they are more enlightened than the rest of us . You too have karma bad

Comments

responded to was in fact displaying the same tone as you targeting men's emotions or trying to trigger men. This video is an example of a lack of humility something you accused this young man of. Part of being a therapist a professional one who attended the best schools and training who went beyond a masters as well, is having empathy for all including those who give you the "ick" your comments were as judgmental as his in addition your advice was unwarranted and unsolicited . Nobody asked for your help so why do you feel the need to give it? Myself ? I never claimed to be holier than thou but I do call out hypocrisy when I see coming from those who do claimed they are more enlightened than the rest of us . You too have karma bad and good albeit and you just accumulated more bad karma with your comment towards this man. You too will answer when you crossover to the spiritual world . And it's not god or the angels forgiveness you need it's this young man's forgiveness you need because you just hurt him. Congratulations, you are nothing more than a human primate just like the rest of us . Good luck 👍

Reply

View 10 more replies

I never got a response from this chick. The man she insulted was basically evaluating a female's attractiveness, calling her average. The female video was a video stating something like low-value men with no money type of thing. It was ridiculous and obviously triggering. There are a lot of "rage bait" reels on Instagram, whether it's a woman-hating or a man-hating topic. People often fall for this trap very easily. Anyway, this old broad seemed gleefully happy "putting this young man in his place," and I was just as gleeful putting her in her place. She had nothing negative to say about this average woman's reel that was degrading to men, but she could not wait to start some shit with a dude who was just giving this creator a piece of her own medicine. So, when I see people starting shit with others, like a spiritual robin hood, I come to the rescue and give the guilty party a piece of their own medicine. This man was innocent, and she decided to be a bitch.

More About Women

Women make a lot of excuses for their lack of action in relationships with men. Are men who abuse women for no good reason responsible for their bad behaviors? Absolutely! Should they change those behaviors? Yep! Now, let me ask you this: In romantic relationships, once a guy shows you he's a dick, and you have an opportunity to escape and never look back, why would you continue the relationship? In addition to that, when there are red flags in the beginning, and there are always red flags with all people when you first meet them, why do you women ignore those flags in the hopes this guy will change? Why do you only see his so-called good and not the major bad he is showing you? More importantly, why do you look over the nerdy, nice guys? Or why do you have kids with shitty men? I can attest to the fact that women, young women especially, become super desperate in romantic relationships. They put romantic relationships on a pedestal; they want this fairy tale romance so badly they will overlook all that bad in men just to be with him. It's almost like women, subconsciously, are attracted to assholes. Maybe there is an evolutionary reason why women are attracted to shitty men. Hmmmm.

Women are raised in a way to value relationships above all else. This is why I say mothers who spend 90% of their time raising children should raise their daughters better. Men do not have power over women's minds to the point they do not show women in the very beginning who they are as people. Women claim men pretend they are great in the beginning. Well, we all put on a great first impression, even on job interviews, but the mistake women make is trusting way too soon without this man proving and backing up what he says with action. Get my point? Employees eventually become comfortable at the workplace after a while, and they truly come to light. (This is why they usually have a 90-day probationary period for new employees). It is the same in any relationship with another human, man or woman. Because women romanticize people, places, and things, they refuse to believe there is any bad in these things, places, and people. Women refuse to look at life as it is. Women look at life how they wish it to be. Women rush into connections with men, give up sex easily, and fall in love with the idea of love, but not the man, only for this man to show who he truly is later, sometimes too late (it's not leaving the man that gets her killed, it's the repeated going back and forth an average of 7 times that gets her killed She can leave the first time, and stay gone, and remain alive-most cases are IPV are not even reported).

It's funny. Women fight more for abortion than they do for stiff consequences for men's bad behaviors. This tells me women aren't serious about what they complain about, and this tells me what the modern woman truly values: casual sex without consequences. Do you want men to treat you poorly? Or do you want other men to protect you? Often, I hear women complain that men, whom they don't know, should be the heroes in violent situations in which women are involved. My philosophy about this is why should someone whom you don't know help you? Why should a stranger who does not rescue people for a living risk their lives for you? It is very selfish of women to expect strange men to assist them in any way. I agree with men here. I, as a woman, would never get involved in a violent situation. I would call the police, though, but I am not physically going to get involved so that I die, too. What good comes from that? One person dead is better than two people dead. Ladies, you seriously lack empathy for other people if you feel strangers should be helping you at all costs, even if those strangers get hurt in the process. How much of a lousy bitch can you be if this is the case? I never expect any stranger to help me with anything, and to be honest, I don't want strangers' help. I can take care of it on my own. If a stranger does help me, I am very appreciative of that, and I express my gratitude; I will never expect a stranger to help, however. That would be self-centered of me to do that. This is how I know women want special treatment and not equality. Men are scared, too; men must worry about other men, too, maybe even women, at times. Do you want to endanger someone else's life for your own personal benefit? And you don't see that as being selfish? If you want equality, learn how to fight off an attacker. Learn self-defense or get a firearm. Men must do the same thing. Not every man is a superhero capable of fighting, and not every man can take on other men. Why would you feel you are deserving of a stranger's help? Who died and made you God? I would not help you either. I need to take care of myself. I also would not expect you to help me in a violent situation. I would want you to be safe. That's a selfless thing to do.

Why can't you protect yourself? Why can't you learn how to be tough, "strong and independent?" Why would a man give up a seat for you when you want equality? Why would a strange man help you in any way when you're "strong and independent?" So, you're only equal when it's convenient for you? So, you value masculinity, but only during times when you selfishly want it? Why do you expect men to hold other men accountable when you're unwilling to hold other women accountable? Equality, remember? How is it a strange man's fault a violent man exists? Why aren't you complaining to that violent man's mother? She was a bad mother, and that's why her son turned out violent. The bad men I've known whose mothers I've met were bad; explains why these men turned out the way they did. These mothers saw their sons as innocent people who did nothing wrong, and it's the rest of the world's fault if the world has a problem with these bad men. You females really destroy us all. Bad men who hurt the planet have assistance in hurting this planet; they have assistance from bad women.

Women make the mistake of thinking they have NO POWER in life whatsoever, even in this so-called patriarchy. You are NOT perpetual victims here. You have the power of choice, thought, and feeling. Stop acting like men have all this control over you like they're the puppeteer and you're the puppet. Because women are at a physical and biological disadvantage over men, women often fear for their safety, especially if these women have been victimized before. So, because of this fear, disadvantage, and biological reality, women tend to place themselves, mentally, in a victimhood type of mode, especially when they're in relationships with men. This is why I say it is very important how you raise your children. It is especially important how mothers model their own behaviors in front of their daughters. With that said, going forward, learn from your mistakes, do better next time, and raise the next generation well. Just because you have been victimized doesn't mean you are a victim. You are human. You are a flawed human who made some mistakes. A vulnerable human (not so strong and independent) who, although has been wronged, needs to acknowledge their role in the situation. There are things you can do to prevent some events from happening again. You do have that power.

SCREW THE MATRIARCHY & PATRIARCHY: LEARN TO WORK AS A TEAM.

Women's advancement, although it had its upsides, came at a cost. Women's advancing left men and boys falling behind. In the USA, the suicide rate is higher for men than it is for women, about 3 or 4 times higher. Young males are failing socially, economically, and educationally compared to their female counterparts. Young men today are three times more likely to overdose, and we all know that most homeless people are male. I am not surprised that a significant number of young men voted for Trump, given these facts about them I just stated. They are feeling left out, lost, ignored, not valued. Most teachers are women, and this is a big problem for boys. The school environment isn't conducive to a young boy's learning style, and I think the genders should be educated separately and differently. In fact, girls are treated better in the school system: Boys are graded unfairly compared to girls ([Discrimination in grading: A scoping review of studies on teachers' discrimination in school - ScienceDirect](#)). Let's not attack masculinity but find a healthy outlet for it. This is why we have school sports, but it seems that isn't enough. So, I am on board with women having equity, but I am not on board with women excluding men from the equation. Men must have a life the way it works for them, not the way it works for you. Men do not want to be women. Allow them to be themselves and accept them how they come. You have no choice. There will always be some semblance of a patriarchy with men's existence. Even in the small matriarchal societies we have now, men are still there. They are still in leadership positions, making decisions that affect everyone ([Friday essay: matrilineal societies exist around the world – it's time to look beyond the patriarchy](#)). This matriarchal society has men in charge of what they do best and women in charge of what they do best. Look into further on your own. They have an EQUITABLE society, NOT AN EQUAL society. It really isn't matriarchy if both genders have power-power in different areas. In a true matriarchy, only women are in charge, and men are submissive. The same with patriarchy. We really have both in the USA. There are situations where women have the upper hand, and there are situations where men have the upper hand. It will never be one or the other in charge when both genders exist. Men are here, and we must learn how to co-exist with them and work alongside them. We must consider how they feel, we need their input, their perspective, etc. Their wants and their desires are just as important or valuable as women's. You have set yourselves back in time because of your incessant need to be in charge, take over, and have complete control. This backfired on you. Now, Trump is president, and it is literally your fault.

Hypocrisy

Humor me this, if the primary caretakers of children are women, then the responsibility of a healthy upbringing of that offspring falls onto the mother's shoulders. (Did you know the most common form of abuse children experience is neglect and emotional abuse vs physical abuse? And guess who is most likely to neglect and emotionally abuse their children? You guessed right. Mothers. Characteristics of perpetrators of child maltreatment | Office of Juvenile Justice and Delinquency Prevention). The reality is single mothers abuse children at a higher rate than when mothers are paired with male partners. In other words, married mothers are least likely to abuse their children. You are at least half responsible for your role in events. Even a therapist will tell a DV survivor that if you do not admit your mistakes if you do not take accountability for your choices and become an active participant in your healing, I will not help you along your journey. It took 12,000 years for women to wake up and become "empowered." Do not expect men to change overnight.

This reminds me of an Instagram comment from a chick who was negative in her assessment of this guy's reel. So, this guy posted a reel trying to encourage men to have compassion for women by picturing their daughters on the receiving end of pain from men. Now, I understood what this chick was saying. She was saying men should just respect women because we're human, and it shouldn't take a man having a close connection to a woman to understand the concept of respect. In other words, a man should not have to have a daughter to have compassion for women, but if you think about it, women tend to understand men better when they have sons. It works both ways. This man's intentions were to try to relay a message to men in a way that men would understand. It might not have been the way this chick wanted it, but it was in a way that might just work

50

and, at the very least, get the ball rolling here. This girl was just so miserable and negative and attacked this poor guy who created such a positive message with a specific goal in mind, and I feel that he has accomplished his goal. This woman made it into some huge political tirade about men and women when the point was to enlighten men on what it is like being a woman. Focus on that. The overall message, not how the message was presented. Thankfully, there were women in the comments who appreciated his video and offered some positive reassurance. As the saying goes, "You can't please 100% of the people 100% of the time." In addition to this male creator, I see other male creators who are self-described "male feminists." These male feminists are still under scrutiny by modern women. I've seen women still complain about these men who are on these women's sides. These modern women are never happy, no matter what a man does, even if that man is trying to help. You ladies have really screwed things up for yourselves. Like a man said to me once, "Make her a Queen; she'll complain about the weight of the crown."

I mention this story because women often expect men to miraculously change 360 degrees to the woman's liking when it literally took 12,000 years for women to get to this point, yet she expects men to "get it," right this minute. The modern woman is so hyper-focused on "getting her way" at all costs, always in every situation. The modern woman is looking to have complete control. This is as toxic as a man having complete control. Neither gender having 100% power is healthy, nor will it work. We can see in the present time and throughout history that this doesn't work. So, this guy's message was very much needed, appreciated, and received well, no matter how he presented it. She should focus on the overall goal in this situation and not those unnecessary details. The more you nag and nitpick men, the less likely they will listen to you or consider your side. You must learn how to get along with them if you expect to coexist peacefully on this planet. I mean, girls, you lost this last election. That should tell you something. That should tell you that you failed somewhere along the way. You should view that as a major red flag about your side of the fence. I mean, women, young men, old men, Latinos, black men, etc, so many groups voted for Trump. You need to pay attention to that. You need to think, gee, where did I go wrong? Something I am doing is not working. Maybe my perception of the world is off. Maybe I do not have a good grasp on reality. These thoughts should be running through your head right now. At this point, we need all hands on deck.

Yin & Yang

I'm not an expert in relationships, but I am smart when it comes to the psychology of human primates; I'm also a big advocate for self-love. Too many relationship gurus out there who are single or have been married not once, not twice, but three times are claiming they know all about what the perfect relationship should look like. That's not me. I know this much: every human wants something in return for their hard work. I'm a huge advocate for the decriminalization of prostitution on a federal level. Okay, fine, at least at a state level. Although, according to science, promiscuity does affect mental health. However, no matter what you do, people will still be people, and the oldest profession in the world will always exist. In addition, sex trafficking could still exist with or without legal prostitution (without strict penalties especially). Still, there is a difference between those who voluntarily choose the profession and those who are forced into it. (DOISerbia - Human trafficking and legalized prostitution in the Netherlands - Siegel, Dina (nb.rs)

It basically boils down to sex. A man's libido, on average, will always be higher than a woman's (Sex difference in libido: Human Andrology (lww.com). So, in other words, men value sex more than women value sex. I'm not making this shit up. This is in our DNA. We're still primates.

The reality is that we are all motivated by pleasure. We do things to get other things in return. We work for money, and that money gives us food, shelter, etc. Some of us may even help a stranger, but that doesn't mean we don't get anything out of it. For some of us, it makes us feel better about helping those in need. It gives us a sense of purpose. Similar to Maslow's Hierarchy of Needs (BEYOND MASLOW'S HIERARCHY OF NEEDS: What Do People Strive For? - ProQuest) - Self-Actualization. I'll even add "Self-Validation."

For example, do people have children for some altruistic reason? No, it's 100% selfish. Having children makes some of us feel better. You're not doing some magical thing here. You're a human primate, and you're selfishly continuing the species to satisfy your own needs and desires without regard to how other people may feel about it. I digress. Having children is a risky move and a scary choice. I personally do not envy your parents at all, especially all the stuff I have witnessed over the years. Having kids is a decision you should not take lightly. There should be some thought behind it. You risk having your kids disown you in later years. Once you're in the nursing home, most of your children will not visit you. This goes for both men and women in nursing homes. I have worked in nursing homes, and the kids rarely visited. This was for various reasons: they hate their parents, or the kids are super busy in their lives. Another new trend is kids disowning their parents - going "no contact." Why have kids when they wind up complaining about every little thing you did in the past? You ladies often choose your kids over your man, which, in some cases, is necessary. Sometimes, you go the opposite extreme and always choose the man. This is why I say it's better to wait until your kids are adults before you date if you're a single parent. However, don't waste a man's time if you're not gonna make him a priority. This critique goes for single dads, too. Sorry, a lot of us don't want to deal with your children, especially since we disagree with how you raise them. Step-parents, unless they have legal control over the kids, never get a say; the biological parent will always assert their authority even though the step-parent is affected by bad decisions. The step-parent is benefitting your child, for you only to undermine your partner. In addition to that, we must deal with the other parents and the drama they bring. No thanks. I will pass.

Research suggested that 45% of women in 2030 will be child-free and single; they might be happy for a short time, but I would love to see the results in the long term. The number of single women

I have spoken to who love their careers say they are quite lonely without a man. I dunno. I have existed this long without kids, and I have never regretted it. I do not know if I could stay single forever though. That is a little different. The fact is that we need people. We need relationships with others, and friends are great, but for a straight woman, you do start to miss the energy of a masculine man in your life after a while. Some relationships can only do so much for you before you start to miss the cuddles, the kisses, the whispers in your ears, and the warm breath grazing your neck. I mean, I don't know, ladies, something about a man's strong hands on our shoulders is enough for me to cream my pants. I do not think these 45% of women will last too long single. My guess is they might start having affairs with those conservative married men they complain about so much but secretly crave their masculine touch. Contrary to popular belief on these social apps, single women are not necessarily the happiest demographic. According to research, only some single women are happy, and only some married women are unhappy. About half the U.S. population is married. Some are obviously happy with their relationships; otherwise, all of them would wanna divorce.

Speaking of masculinity, women shouldn't complain about men not being masculine when they are unwilling to be in their feminine. Let him take the lead. Men pursue or chase. Women are supposed to be on the receiving end.

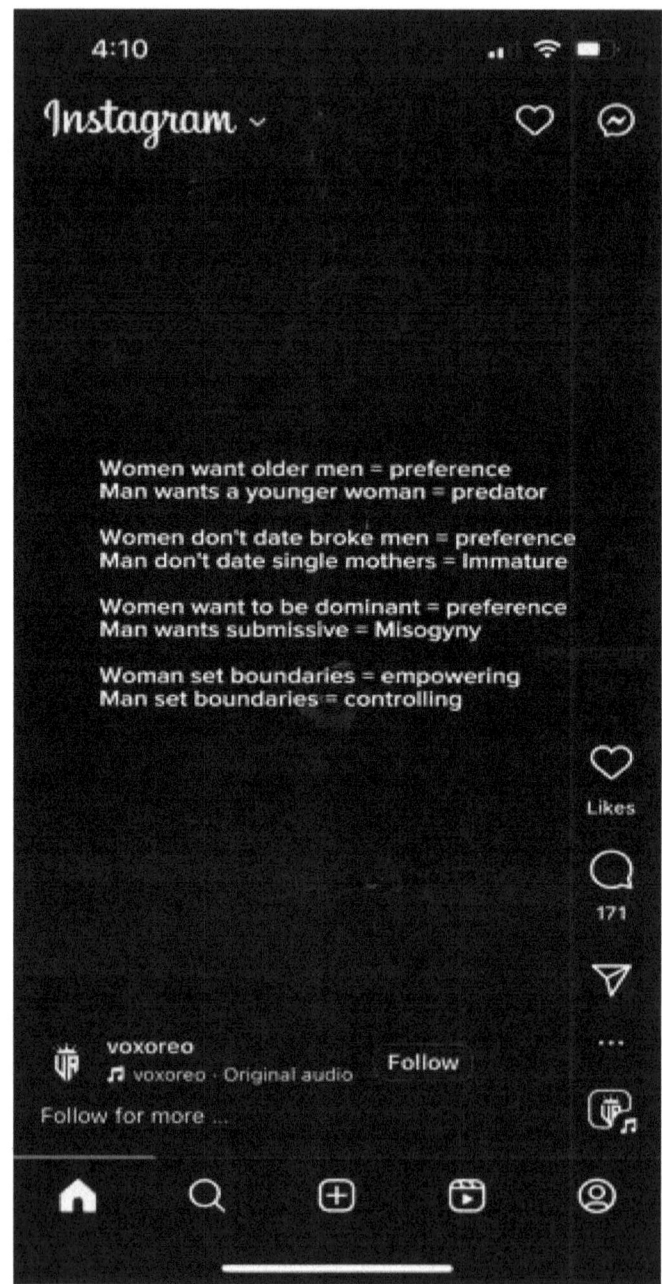

The reality is that we haven't changed much since cave times. I can tell we haven't because now, women are complaining about modern men being too feminine and not masculine enough. LOL. This is super comical to me because, on the one hand, you ladies want to be in charge so badly, and then on the other hand, you want men to take the lead. I mean, which is it? You can't have a modern man and a traditional man all at once. You pay for the dinner date. You plan a date night with your husband. You initiate sexual encounters. Why should he do these things all the time? I say the same thing to men: you can't have a modern woman (50/50) and then have a traditional woman at the same time. It doesn't work that way. We are in an era where some of the old ways are dying off and overlapping the new ways. Women say this is where equality comes in. I say to you I have just proved, so far, that what you ladies really want is SPECIAL TREATMENT, not equality. True equality means you must be exactly like men and vice versa, and this is impossible. True equality means you also must be held accountable for your role in relationships. How did you contribute to the downfall of marriage? What did you do wrong, not just your husband? That's 50/50! (What you should be asking for is EQUITY). You want the man to plan dates, that's very masculine of him, so what is the feminine thing you are doing? Or you can plan the dates. In addition to that, do you want to date and emotionally connect? At what point do you plan on having sex in exchange for that emotional connection? It is not dating nor romance without the sex. No sex means platonic friends. Sex is exactly what makes a situation romantic. You can emotionally connect with your female friends, too. Why are you dating if you plan NOT to have sex? That's not logical.

The number of married men I've heard call their wives roommates instead of the love of their lives, their lovers, or their sweethearts, just cause they ain't fucking is crazy. You want your husband to listen to you, but when do you plan on listening to him? Men often tell me when they do open up to you women, you use their words against them. They often say you do not consider how they feel. Remember, your empathy must expand beyond women, children, and the vulnerable. You also must have empathy for the people you perceive as having the upper hand. Are they not human? Are they not worthy of love as well? This is what happens when bad mothers, most modern women, do not raise their daughters in preparation for adult life. You ladies basically do the bare minimum: food, water, and shelter. You need to go beyond that when raising children. Model the type of behavior you want to see from your kids. You should be the type of woman you want your daughters to be. You basically teach your daughters that they are perfect little princesses who can do no wrong; you protect them from all pain because, God forbid, a girl falls off her bike and gets a bruise or a job and pays for her own cell phone at 14 years old. So, when you broads become adult women, you feel entitled to special treatment.

Heterosexual Dating

I have learned a few things along the way when I was dating, and here is a list of strategies I've considered.:

I choose intelligence, or at least someone on my intellectual level. Anything below my intelligence will bore me. Also, having high intelligence will make him think twice before cheating because he will think about the consequences of cheating. Why? Because he would know how costly it would be for him if he cheated. Intelligence doesn't necessarily mean being formally educated. I have come across many who have no degrees, but when tested, it is discovered they have a higher-than-average IQ.

High moral compass. This coincides with spiritual or religious beliefs. Men who have morals are least likely to cheat, value love, not just sex, and are more than likely to give you a long-term commitment. You free-loving liberals ruined morality. That free sex movement backfired on women. Now, all men want is sex because they can get it without committing. Men should not determine marriage. You should. In some ways, I feel you should wait until marriage before sex. Some of the old-school values have merit. I am partial to men who have some sort of spiritual beliefs. If they put that higher power first, they are least likely to hurt you, least likely to be sexually perverse, more than likely to take you seriously and end up giving you a commitment.

Masculinity. Women want to feel protected and cared for by men. No matter how "independent" a woman is in life, she still wants her protector. Effeminate men will have you fight off an attacker. Good luck with that. I do not do 50/50. Roommates go 50/50. Men take the lead and provide. I am traditional, and if you're not, that's your business. I am also not asking for equality. That's the modern feminist's department. I am not interested in building bridges or fixing cars. It's great if you are, but I am not. I want to be treated like a lady, hold the door open, pull out my chair, fight off an attacker, etc. If you are a woman, you are more than welcome to lead all you want. If you are a man, you are more than welcome to allow the woman to be the man in the relationship. I mean, if you want to get pegged, just say that. Again, that's your business. But do not judge people who prefer a different relationship dynamic. Especially since research indicates women who lead in marriages have higher failure rates than in marriages where the men lead. Find the right people for you. I never trust a man who makes me lead. That's very feminine of him and a major turn-off. On the first couple of dates, sure, I will pay my own way; however, once I commit, the man pays. If I pay half the bills, okay, then it goes half my way, and I will behave masculine, just like you. If you want me to be feminine, you need to be masculine. Period. Be prepared to add to someone's life. Otherwise, your presence is unnecessary. Some of us aren't so desperate that we will go for the bottom-of-the-barrel effort.

I want to expand on this first or second date thing when it comes to who pays. I put myself in the man's shoes after a conversation with a man I had about who pays for dates, and I understood what men were talking about and how they felt. See? Empathy works both ways. Let me break this down. You're a man who gets rejected over and over by women. You have very good intentions with these women, and you come across as the "nice guy," but maybe you're being rejected over and over because you're ugly or a little effeminate, shy, introverted, etc. Masculinity, social skills, and taking the lead are what will draw women in. No matter what a woman says about this, she's a fucking liar. Back to the man being rejected over and over. So, imagine you're being rejected, no matter how hard you try, then factor in going on dates where you are paying the entire bill. Life is expensive; restaurants and various social events are expensive – you can be paying 100-500 dollars depending on where you are going.

You, as the man, could spend anywhere from 500-1000 a month on dates, dating more than one woman, but each woman rejects you one after the other. How would you feel? We are all in a financial pinch, and you mean to tell me you have NO EMPATHY at all for men who are spending hard-earned money on women only to be rejected in the end just because he was too shy? Why should he pay for you and him if he risks the chance of being rejected? You should absolutely pay your own way until if, and only if, you two are committed. Now I know why men would flip out after I rejected them when they paid for the date. I should have paid my own way. So, common courtesy would be to pay for yourself, EQUALITY, RIGHT? Pay for yourself; that way, the man cannot feel entitled to you in anyway, and if you reject him, he will feel not much was lost on his side of things. That would be the considerate thing to do. Now, that's a feminine woman - a woman who considers how other people feel, especially how men feel.

Onto Sex. Compatibility in this area is super important! (Infidelity and Its Associated Factors: A Systematic Review | The Journal of Sexual Medicine | Oxford Academic (oup.com) I need to be on the same page as a man when it comes to sex. Incompatibility is a major contributor to short term romances and infidelity, in my opinion. If you aren't interested in sex all that much, if you're not adventurous in the bedroom, and if you don't make an effort to keep up an attractive appearance, you risk having your man cheat on you. Just know going into it, sex is majorly important to most men. Just know your men hide their true fantasies from you for fear of being rejected or shamed. Men should also realize that they risk not getting sex when they want it, how often, and how they want it when dealing with women. Women are wired differently. If you men can't accept that, date other men instead. Compromise, people. Some men are wired to like variety. They like different types of women, different types of sexual experiences, and so on. Sometimes, you will never be enough, and you might not be his ideal. He settles for you just like you settle for him. You also have the choice of dating an asexual man who wants little to no sex at all.

There are a lot of cheaters out there, and the number one complaint I hear from men is that there is "no sex in the relationship." I saw a reel about a woman, who obviously was cheated on before, complaining about the mistress of her ex-husband. It was hilarious. Never blame the other woman. The other, more attractive woman is not responsible for your relationship, nor is she obligated to be nice to you, especially since you are half responsible for your relationship. You're supposed to be having sex with your husband. You had sex while dating, so why is being married different suddenly? I remember one time a wife said to me, in front of her husband, who was making passes at me, "Where's your husband?" I replied, "I don't need one. I have yours." They later divorced. Now, she's old, used up, single, and lonely. Her kids hate her and blame her for the divorce. Yowzers. Maybe fuck your man next time?

If you happen to be "the other woman," never feel guilty. You're probably the "better" woman in the situation. It's impossible to break up a happy home. If the home was happy, no outsider would have a chance. He does not divorce because of the money and property that he will lose, as well as the childcare and domestic support his wife provides. Men also do not want to lose access to their kids. In custody cases, over 60% of full custody is given to the woman. We all know how women use their kids as pawns against their exes after divorcing. I talked to one guy online who said he was waiting until his daughter turned 18 before initiating the divorce. His wife was a "career" woman, always busy; he was lonely and in a sexless marriage. I am glad I don't have these problems. It's super important to choose spouses wisely, folks.

Side Note About Marriage & Parenthood

I do not feel anyone should receive alimony. If you are not contributing to your marriage anymore, you do not deserve the benefits of marriage. You failed as a wife or husband, and you should go back to how your life was before the marriage. Those houses women get are not deserved (more single women own homes than single men BECAUSE ladies you TAKE these homes from the divorce. Only 13% of single women own homes. That's not a lot. Out of that 13%, a large portion are women who have stolen those homes from their ex-husbands through divorce. Most homes are owned by couples or entire families). They failed as wives. Nowadays, you can make money online, so when the modern woman talks about women not being able to survive post-divorce unless she was working, I laugh because explain to me the alimony and homes women receive after divorce. Nowadays, SAHMs can work online at home. In addition, a lot of male providers financially support their wives who want to start their own businesses. So, being a successful SAHM is quite possible. I've known women who stayed at home while their kids were young; then, they went back to work when the kids got older. Their marriages were very successful, and their kids turned out normal. If these women can do it, so can you.

I laugh when I hear women say the labor they provided was unpaid labor that should be compensated. I say, well, you CHOSE that labor. You should have known going into the marriage what the situation would be like. You AGREED to be a mother. You AGREED to get married and forego a career. This was your willingness to engage in this lifestyle. You are NOT owed money for something you willingly agreed to. I'm glad I'm not a man who has to put up with this shit. I feel for you, gentlemen. One thing I find hilarious is that women consider motherhood labor they want to be paid for. This is ridiculous. You know the old saying "a labor of love?"

That is exactly how I feel about parenting. If you love children, especially your own children, it's not labor. If you don't love being a mother, and it's a chore for you, you really should not be a mother. I enjoy cooking. I can cook all day and not get paid because it brings me so much joy. Even if I have no one to cook for, I will still cook for myself. Being on my feet for hours does not concern me, nor does it bother me because I get so much happiness from cooking. This is how I feel if you are a mother who really loves her children. Your kids can sense when you are unhappy, and it comes across as they are an inconvenience to you. You hurt your children when you sign up for a situation you didn't want in the first place. Maybe schools should give a trial run to kids to see how they would like to be a parent before they decide that path.

I talk to single dads who have physical custody, and they never complain about being a parent. In fact, they say they enjoy their kids. It's fun for them. They even say the work involved is easy, even when they work outside the home simultaneously. These single dads manage their time wisely and do not stress over unimportant little things, as women do; they make it work. I never hear men complain or brag about being a single dad, and I never hear people, especially women, admire, appreciate, or congratulate single dads, who do most or all of the work. These men are successful in their careers and home lives. I've dated two single dads. They might not have been compatible partners for me, but they were very good fathers. The mothers of their kids, well, that's another story. We won't go there. LOL. Why are you single mothers so bad at this? Women must experience more negative emotions than men, if women are so easily overwhelmed with parenthood. Most American women are just not cut out to be mothers. I feel most of you should just stay on birth control or don't have sex, please. You are doing a disservice to future generations and the people who are already here who must put up with your miserable attitude and the pain from your kids whose lives you ruined.

Back To Sex…

Being online a lot, I've noticed that there are a lot of men who entertain other women while being married or partnered. If sex is a chore for you, or you have some aversion towards sex for whatever reason, stay away from men. When you're sick or pregnant and not fucking, your men might cheat. If you're sick, give your man a hall pass, at least for a day. Don't be selfish, especially if he is paying the bills. I knew a guy whose wife couldn't have intercourse; this guy worked his fingers to the bone while she got to stay home and do nothing. Their kids were grown, and she couldn't even get her lazy ass up to give her husband a blow job. She ignored him and acted like he wasn't wanted, valued, or desired. My lord, I have met so many women not working after their kids are grown and not contributing to the marriage and household, this includes being a loving wife to your husband. What's wrong with you? How selfish can you be? This is how I know women want special treatment and not equality.

These online men hold many secrets. They confessed so many things to me because I did not judge them (I was gathering research for this manuscript). Your men are into other men, animals, children, spit, shit, piss, their relatives, etc. The list goes on. You ladies are clueless about what happens when you're asleep, or at work, or at the grocery store, or when your man is hiding in the bathroom, wherever. I felt bad for one guy who works hard and pays the bills; the wife gets to play hopscotch all day with the kids and never works. She should give her husband a break and let him fuck someone else. Other men get their sex but want something different for a day. I wound up counseling these men because I truly felt bad for some of them. Some of them were not bad guys. I saw men differently during this time. I saw their being vulnerable. Some just wanted a companion, someone to talk to every now and then. There are even Muslim men online doing things they shouldn't be doing. I convinced one Muslim, during Ramadan, to focus on God and not pussy. He said to me, "You're right."

Sexuality makes a difference for straight women. Only straight men for me. I am straight, so it makes sense I will only be compatible with other straight people. I cannot relate to the Rainbow. "Taste the Rainbow." LOL. You have the option of having an effeminate man by your side. Like, a super feminine dude. So, like bisexual or very submissive. However, there is a good reason why straight women don't want bisexual men; you're whores. Men, both gay and straight, have very high libidos, tend to be less safe, and take more risks, and men who have sex with other men are the number one transmitter of HIV infections (CDC.gov). "It's not bigotry if it's reality." Date your own kind, other bisexuals. Straight people are turned off by homosexuality simply because they're straight! Duh! It's not bigotry if it's reality. It's also a rational fear to worry about gay men, who are oversexualized, spreading diseases then passing them onto you, as well as the fear of being cheated on, as it is easier for men to get other men to sleep with them than it is to get women to sleep with them. A bisexual will never be sexually satisfied with just one woman for life. He needs some semblance of homosexuality in the bedroom, and that turns women off. No, I do not want to peg you in the ass. Gross. I'm not a dude, nor do I want to be like a dude. There are so many men online who pretend to be straight but are down-low gay. I talked to a guy online who was married to a woman, cheated on her with trannies, who are just men in dresses. His wife had no idea. This married couple both traveled for business, a lot. He said the reason why he slept around was because he liked the variety. I said why lie to your wife and then be married in the first place? He said, "Well, you know how it is." LOL. Wow. Yowzers. Interesting how he decided to marry a real woman and not a tranny. Are you ashamed about being attracted to trannies? You trans will never get a straight man's commitment. You are a perverse side piece, at best.

You must be a priority. I never take a back seat to the children, mother-in-law, or any female relative. Mama's boys get kicked to the curb. I'm the one doing the hard work of performing blowjobs on that sucker; I come before others. My perfect match feels the same way. However, who will ever find that "perfect" match in reality? I don't date single dads anymore (I understand why men do not want to date single mothers). You will never be a priority. Single parents should wait until their kids are adults before they date anyone. Your time should go towards your kids; I agree. However, they are not my kids, and I don't want to put time, money, or effort into them. I need your time, however, and I deserve it. I'm not doing work, and you get to do nothing in return. In the Christian bible, God says the spouse comes before the children and mother-in-law. My point has been made.

Betrayal

If you're with a man for 9 years, no ring, and you even go so far as to have his kids for him, you're nothing more than a placeholder. He kept you around, waiting for something better. When better doesn't come along, he settles for you. All the while, he probably cheated without your knowing. I never understood why women did not require marriage before children. Your fault if you become disappointed, in this case. We women consider everything cheating: flirting, looking at other women, looking at girls online, adding random girls as friends on Facebook, etc. I talked to this one guy who told me he used to tell his ex-wife when he was about to watch porn. Lmao. Omg. First, what a sissy. "Mommy, just to let you know, I'm gonna watch Brazilian face sitting. Is that okay with you? Tee Hee. I'm so bashful." When a woman says she doesn't care about your watching porn, bullshit, she cares.

Open relationships don't necessarily last long, and they're not particularly better relationships. I looked up the results of polyamorous relationships, and I found out they aren't any better than monogamous relationships. Same outcomes, good or bad. I also found out straight women are the least likely to be on board with poly lifestyle. The group most likely interested are, you guessed it, MEN! Both hetero and homosexual. Yep, no surprise there. Next on the list are bisexual women and lesbian women. Yeah, sorry, I do not go for multiple partners. Not my bag. Too much drama and I'm not into sleeping with more than one person at a time. Way too much work. I see a lot of younger women tolerating this poly/hook-up nonsense from their male partners, only to be disappointed when he does not emotionally connect with them nor commit for the long term. Women naturally want love and commitment, and straight women hate poly. In practice, people are just having sex, no emotional intimacy present, no loyalty, no dedication. It is superficial. When I tell women online all of this about men, they say, all the time, "Not my man." I laugh hysterically. Yes bitch, your man too. I had to prove to this one chick on Facebook that her man was a cheater. Here is the story:

Social Experiment

I did a social experiment, as I do often with the human primate, just for shits & giggles. I said, let me catch taken men cheating. So, I added random men on Facebook, under a troll account, to see who would flirt with me and even maybe go further. (I should do this for a living) Now, I don't look like anything special at all; however, men really don't care, ladies. If they are willing to fuck anything, men, animals, holes in the drywall, they would be willing to fuck me. Pussy is pussy, to a lot of men, and they do not like missing opportunities for sex, especially if they like variety. A guy told me once, "No man has ever died wishing he got less pussy."

One of the guys I added was a black man (black men lust after light skin and light eyes, which is what I have. They foam at the mouth like rabid dogs over light skin and light eyes). He and I flirted privately. I sent pictures. He sent pictures. I went to his page to see if I saw a woman in his life. Guess what? He had a girlfriend. I would post replies to his comments, and I would see her in comments looking suspicious, like, "Who is this chick." I laughed. She gave him way too much attention, totally up his ass; he DID NOT return that same energy she gave, a sign of a user and a cheater. Eventually, she found out, and he acted like he didn't like me in front of her. They both attacked me through messages. I stood my own, insult after insult, taking them down, word for word. Guess what? After this, she messaged me to say, "Thank you." You know why? She found out he was cheating on her offline with his ex-girlfriend. He was using his current girlfriend for money. This brotha "didn't have a pot to piss in nor a window to throw it out," as my father used to say. I can always tell a cheater a mile away. A big sign was this guy was hot, and she was not. Like a smart girl, she dumped him.

A man freshly divorced, I stay away. He ain't ready. All he has to offer is sex. He just got out of a marriage; he ain't gonna commit anytime soon, or if at all. On average, the second marriages end quicker than the first. As I am writing this, some married dude made a pass at me last week. Claimed he was going through a divorce, yet he admitted to not having filed. LOL. Your husbands are cheaters and hit on the rest of us a lot. Now, I would not forgive cheating, but some women would forgive men's infidelity. I mean, that's their choice, and I won't judge because maybe that man offers a whole bunch of stuff in return, and that woman does not want to lose those things. It's a personal choice if you want to forgive someone. Me? Never. Nope. You're out. As far as you married men, sorry, you're not getting it. In the words of Ray Liotta in the movie *Good Fellas*, "Fuck you, pay me."

Sex, sex, and more sex. What women need and will *always* need is to feel SAFE around a man. We need to feel that comfort. We also need an emotional connection to get horny[1] (on average). Some gurus on TikTok said to wait 3 months for sex with no exclusivity because it takes 3 months for people to show their true colors. This same guru's man made her make a 40k deposit before she moved in with him. Yowzers. In addition to that, I watched these two in a car on a live TikTok video. She did all the talking, one random topic to the next, non-stop babbling, it was annoying and super draining. Her man had a look on his face like, "Please shut the fuck up." He wasn't engaging in the conversation at all, and he seemed totally uninterested in her as a person. Yeah, I'm not taking her advice. I do not need the three-month rule because it doesn't take me all but one minute to figure a man out. I'm super smart and discerning. I pay attention to everything, and in my experience, men show who they

---

[1] Wood, Wendy, and Alice H. Eagly. "2 Biosocial Construction of Sex Differences and Similarities in Behavior." *Advances in experimental social psychology* 46.1 (2012): 55-123.

are right away. It's too much work for them to pretend, even beyond a week, that they're Prince Charming. You broads aren't as smart if you use the excuse men put on an act. I find they don't. You're just not paying attention, you're desperate, and you don't love yourself. You are also not listening to your intuition. I like what Maya Angelou said, "When someone shows who they are, believe them."

Here are some pictures of conversations and men's profiles on dating apps. I used myself as a guinea pig to show you how easy this is done. Men are easy to figure out quickly. It takes no time at all to be good at this, and what I find with women is they don't love themselves enough, and they tolerate a lot from men. Men should also be discerning, especially when looking for a mother for their kids. She might be good in bed, but would she make a good wife and mother? Yeah, she's hot, but will she bring you peace? She's fun and accommodating in the beginning, but you should wait a few months and see how she behaves during a conflict or a challenge. She may say she is a Christian and puts God first, but how does she treat other people, especially other women, who look better than her? Does she get jealous easily? Does she criticize other females unfairly? How she interacts with other women is how she will interact with your daughter. How godly and holy is she? Is she gentle with the world and in the world? Or is she a brute of a beast and quite aggressive? Unless all you want is sex, then never mind. Hump a wall.

well, yes lol

Video Call available

Looks like you're having a nice conversation. Why not talk face-to-face?

Try Video Call →

? what is your ideal kind of guy or partner

What brought you to my profile?

Well, I'm not fond of giving men a map to my panties lol I'll know who my soulmate is when I meet him. Just be yourself.

I'm new to this dating life and just want to see what's out here

I see.

I'm the kind of guy that wants to see where your head and heart is and try to feel a vibe between the both of us

Well, you may ask questions about

+ 🎁   Message

74

What brought you to my profile?

Well, I'm not fond of giving men a map to my panties lol I'll know who my soulmate is when I meet him. Just be yourself.

I'm new to this dating life and just want to see what's out here

I see.

I'm the kind of guy that wants to see where your head and heart is and try to feel a vibe between the both of us

Well, you may ask questions about me , I'll answer

have you been married before

Never been married. You?

right now as we speak I am going through a divorce of 13yr

Oh wow

divorce will be final February next year

+ 🎁 Message 💬 🎤

divorce will be final February
next year

we had no kids together

> So that in combo with your profile
> saying short term, you want
> casual .

I take it you have no kids correct

> No kids

> I do not do casual. I date to marry.
> Looking for my last.

I'm just looking if anything
happened I'll just let nature takes
its course

I'm not looking for casual

> I see

so what you do for work

> Well your profile says short term
> what do you mean by that ?

> I manage a group hor

Message

I disagree with you

It's better to be single than miserable

I apologize you're correct

You do ?

Interesting

No need to apologize those are your
True
Thoughts

It's good that I know so I act accordingly

See why I don't give a map ? lol

I see

lol

We're not on the same mindset so I'm gonna pass you by but good luck to you

thank same to you

+ 🎁 Message   🎤

to tell

Compatibility is necessary otherwise time is wasted and hearts are broken when that perfect mate was passed on by while wasting time with the wrong one

I disagree with you

It's better to be single than miserable

I apologize you're correct

You do ?

Interesting

No need to apologize those are your
True
Thoughts

It's good that I know so I act accordingly

See why I don't give a map ? lol

I see

Message

Unpopular opinion

 Eugenics is a good idea

About me

Funny. Smart. Empathetic.

Looking for my Soulmate.

I date to marry

General info

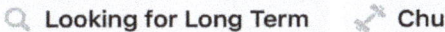

🔍 Looking for Long Term   Chubby

Childfree   🐾 I don't have any pets

🍷 Socially   Socially   🍴 No diet

Religion: Other   Height: 5'4''

🅰 Speak English   Moderate

Interests

😂 Stand-up   Museum

Martial Arts   🏈 Football

🧁 Cooking/Baking   🐈 Cat lover

Q   Figuring out my dating goals

&   Figuring out my relationship type

Life of the party

eave a comment...

out Jay

e today like there is no tomorrow

neral info

Looking for Short Term, Open to Long

Chubby

Have kid(s) not ready for more

I don't ha pets Socially

Never No diet

General info

Looking for Short Term, Open to Long

Chubby

Have kid(s), not ready for more

I don't have any pets   Socially

Never   No diet

Height: 5'7"   Speak English

Unpopular opinion

 Eugenics is a good idea

About me

Funny. Smart. Empathetic.

Looking for my Soulmate.

I date to marry

General info

Looking for Long Term   Chubby

Childfree   I don't have any pets

Socially   Socially   No diet

Religion: Other   Height: 5'4''

Speak English   Moderate

Interests

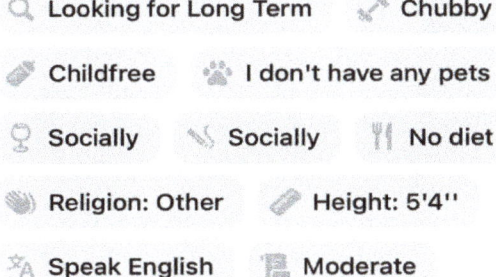

😂 Stand-up   🖼️ Museum

🥋 Martial Arts   🏈 Football

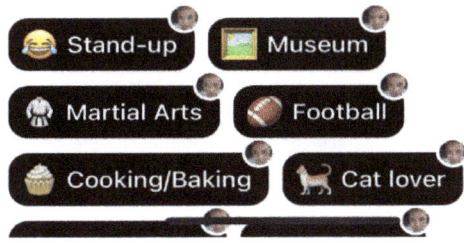

🧁 Cooking/Baking   🐈 Cat lover

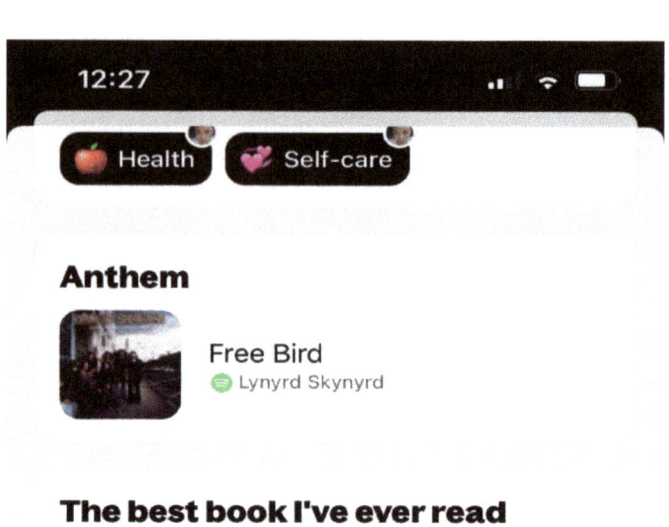

Health Self-care

Anthem

Free Bird
Lynyrd Skynyrd

The best book I've ever read

Iron John By Robert Bly

One thing I would never do is

Give men a map to my panties. lol don't
ask me who is my ideal man. Be
yourself.

Verification

Mobile number   Photo

Back to top

In this example, I should not have revealed much of anything about what I was looking for right away. I should have just asked questions and let him do all the talking. Let them talk up a storm; they will reveal a lot right away. As you can see, the biggest red flag with men's profiles is "looking for short term." Even if they are open to commitment if you take a chance, they still will not commit to you but to someone else who they feel is worthy of their commitment. So, to be on the safe side, block men who say "short term." Sometimes, they will not commit to anyone. Always bypass these profiles right away. You see, in one of the profiles, the guy didn't know what he wanted. I don't know why the app even has these options, but they do offer them. Seems like an app geared towards men and rainbow people. At the end of the day, I am still a woman, as you can see from the way I was interacting with this dude. Women want commitment right away. We know what we want. You must find a guy who literally says, "I date to marry" in his profile. Even if they say they want a relationship, they could just say that to get some pussy because they know that's what you want to hear. See, if all women were on the same page, making men wait for sex, men would be less into short term and more into long term. Because men are so used to women allowing free sex, men will move on quickly if they can't get that free pussy right away because they know there will always be a female willing to give it up who has low self-esteem. Culturally, society needs to value marriage, love, and commitment. This is why the Western world has problems between genders. Commitment should be controlled by the woman, not the man, by withholding pussy until marriage, as they do in Middle Eastern countries.

Just to let you know, some people are just better than you - better looking, smarter, or more likable as people. A lot of you ladies are low on the beauty scale yet so picky about men. I am guilty of it myself. I get it; it's our biology to be picky, but if you really want a man in your life, you must stick with the average guy. I tried to hook up this 50-something-year-old woman with a guy online. She was super out of shape. Naturally a bad body shape anyway, was fat, old as hell, and did not look like she aged well at all. She was very ugly, had bad hair, and the list goes on. She had the nerve to say the guy I was trying to hook her up with was not her physical type. She wasn't attracted to him. Without even reading his profile or getting to know him, she rejected him right away. I said, "What? He is literally on your physical attractiveness level." He seemed like a nice guy, said he wanted to be in love, etc. Women are just as superficial and nonsensical as men. I do not ever want to hear a woman complain about men's standards when this chick rejects a perfectly great guy who is on the exact same level as her. Sweetheart, the above-average men are reserved for the above-average women. Men do this same shit. Men are really concerned with looks, so ladies, you do not qualify for someone so high on the food chain. Stop reaching out of your league. The more successful and good-looking the man, the pickier he is about whom he wants by his side. The healthier the man, the pickier he is about his woman. The more substance a man has, the more substance you must have. You ladies are super unaware and unrealistic when it comes to yourselves. A lot of you will have to settle for 3rd or 4th best or just stay single. My guess would be you ladies are also 3rd or 4th best. I say this same shit to men, who often reach way too high on the beauty scale, and I am sorry, there is a conventional beauty standard. We all usually agree on who is attractive and who isn't generally. Beauty is not in the eye of the beholder. Some people are downright ugly, and we can all agree with that.

Now, look at this convo I had with this "brotha." (I attract a lot of black men. I will talk about them later. They should stick with their own kind). We will call him Tyrone (not his real name, and yes, I am being funny). He said he wanted to get into my mind and heart to see if we vibe right after he asked me who my ideal man would be. If he was genuine about getting into my heart and mind, he would have mentioned a few things in my profile that were very interesting. I mean, he would have been intrigued and would want to know more about me. Never answer the question "What kind of guy do you like?" because they want to know how to get into your pants by pretending to be the guy they know you want. This charade doesn't last for long because like I said, men don't want to do all this work in pretending to be prince charming; they give up and show their true colors right away. This is why you make them wait a decent amount of time for sex. That's why that guru said 3 months. Again, for me, it doesn't take 3 months to figure a man out because, as you can see within a few sentences, I rejected Tyrone right away.

He said all the wrong things. His profile said short term, and he highlighted he didn't have kids with his soon-to-be ex-wife because he saw in my profile that I do not have kids and do not want them, and my ideal man has no kids. I changed this in my profile. See? I made a mistake and gave him a heads-up. Although, in his profile, he said he had kids, so, they must be from a previous relationship. Never give a man a heads-up on what type of man you like. Always answer by saying, "Just be yourself; I will let you know if I like you." You also noticed his statement about waiting for the right one, and I said I disagreed with him. He apologized, like, for what, dude? LOL, why? He wants this pussy, that's why. He will agree with me just to get this pussy, by any means necessary. As soon as he said he was going through a divorce, I should have unmatched. In fact, I should not have responded at all since he has kids, and I am not compatible with someone who has kids. See the fat guy with the description, "Party animal, and short term?" Bye, fat guy. He just wants to play and doesn't take anything seriously; plus, he didn't shave in his picture, and he didn't look like he took good care of himself. Some guys focus too much on their looks, which makes them appear ultrafeminine. I want to mention men who say they are looking for an "open-minded, spontaneous woman." This translates to, "I am a weird freak with sex. Sex is my priority, and I am also a gay dude who is into getting pegged." Look at his picture: earrings, tons of jewelry, well-done eyebrows, and feminine features. Pass this queer on by. Oh, men who give duck faces in pics are super gay. These young men also use face filters, just like girls. Yuck. What's wrong with this young generation? Jesus.

I must have rejected hundreds of thousands of men online, and I don't look like anything special, and I'm old. According to some men, my dating score has now decreased (laugh out loud). Other than women having baggage and this "high body count" thing, I see why men say this: as women get older, they become more rigid, less flexible both physically and mentally, bitter, tired, less fun, hard to get along with, all the above. I can attest to this because I have always had issues with women older than I am. Also, there is scientific evidence of what happens to the brain as it ages. Our brains do become more rigid, less novel, etc. I ask men why they do not want women their age, and they tell me that other than not being able to have kids, these older women are "mean." Also, the older women get, the likelihood their libido decreases. Sex is important in romantic relationships, and men do not want to waste their time if there is little to no sex. What's wrong with sex in a committed relationship, ladies? Older women tend to be no fun, not lively, not laid back, and not full of life, especially if they have health issues. I can say similar things about older men as well. I have had a cougar stage, and I can tell you I understood men during this time. The positive thing about younger people is that they don't stress the small stuff. They are a lot of fun and more accommodating; they are least likely to argue with you over nonsense, not bitter, rarely angry about life, they don't have baggage, etc. So, I get why men want younger women. Older women get upset at this, but honey, there are logical reasons why sometimes younger people are more appealing partners. These older women are just jealous. Nowadays, I see more older women going younger, so maybe you gals should stop being jealous or bitter and go out there and get you a "cub." You need some good sex in your life to calm your uptight asses down.

You need to stop looking at life with rose colored glasses, being swayed by sweet talk and the simple exchanges of pleasantries. Look at yourselves objectively. Look at yourself how a man would look at you. Men want feminine, agreeable, easy to get along with, etc. and a few other things, but if you don't fit this, you will have to settle. You may not understand a man's standards, and they might not make sense to you because you're a woman! To a man, it's reasonable. Just like you, men are allowed to have requirements. Why does this upset you? Then you judge men for getting upset at your requirements? Realistically, most of us are average and only qualify for average. That means something: We will not get every box checked off our list. So, I say this with love: lower your requirements. I say the same to men: lower your beauty standards and body count standards. You are delusional if you think you are the perfect woman or man. You are average, and looks are not enough for a man to give a woman a commitment. Having a career is not important to a lot of masculine men (effeminate men might love the idea of a career woman, but not so much with a masculine man). So, you have a job. Big deal. So do men. So, you majored in Feminist Studies or Gender Studies. Big whoop. Men are in the Tech Fields making real change, yet they don't brag about that. Without men, you wouldn't have electricity, roads to drive on, or a toilet to flush. The gender most likely dominating these things is men. What can Gender Studies do for a society? So, you're an overpaid CEO, okay? Your job is worthless, like all CEOs. At best, that's a minimum-wage job. People who do the real work are at the bottom. Stop thinking you are God's gift to humanity. Someone might have a different opinion about you.

The Great Stuff About Men

There are some things I like and admire about men. It's a nice feeling, coming from a woman, to have a man protect us. Again, it's within our nature to feel safe. Men are very useful in a lot of situations. When I want a straightforward, no-bullshit answer without the extra sentences women tend to provide, I ask a straight man. Women are prone to this type of bullshit communication, communication that is intricate and convoluted[2]. In my opinion, men, on average, have a better sense of direction. I'm sorry, ladies, but men are better drivers (iii). I must disagree with the finance guy at the dealership[3]. The majority of my car accidents were caused by women. Women tend not to have courage on the road, and they are too cautious. They are easily prone to making costly mistakes on the road. Decide, ya dumb broad, left or right? Men might be more aggressive and riskier, but at least they are better skilled at driving. I agree that there are horrible men out there, and most violent crimes are committed by men. (Explaining gender differences in crime and violence: The importance of social cognitive skills - ScienceDirect) However, what kind of mothers did these men have? You know how many single mothers I've seen that beat the hell out of their sons in public? Remember, single mothers abuse their children at higher rates than partnered mothers. No wonder why a lot of men have issues with women. When will these women be held accountable just

---

[2] Campellone, Timothy R., and Ann M. Kring. "Context and the Perception of Emotion in Schizophrenia: Sex Differences and Relationships with Functioning." *Schizophrenia research* 149.0 (2013): 192–193. *PMC*. Web. 4 Nov. 2016.

[3] Piccardi L, Matano A, D'Antuono G, et al. Persistence of Gender Related-Effects on Visuo-Spatial and Verbal Working Memory in Right Brain-Damaged Patients. *Frontiers in Behavioral Neuroscience*. 2016; 10:139. doi:10.3389/fnbeh.2016.00139.

like men are held accountable? Know that women are half responsible for the problems in this world. This is a fact. Equality, right? You want equal rights but not equal responsibility? Doesn't work that way. Ladies, take responsibility for your choices. You ladies are more powerful than you think. You hold the weight of the world, and even though there is no world without your consent, currently, you still need sperm.

Other things I like about men: They are not petty unless they're gay. When I speak about men here, I am talking about what you freaky libbies call 'cis, straight men.' They're just men, you idiots. Enough with the non-sensical descriptors; they are making life more difficult for everyone! Anyway, yes, men do not offer those little jabs, like extra, unnecessary comments women and gays do all the time. Then, these people wonder why they're hated. I would argue that straight men have more empathy and compassion than women and gays. I get along best with straight men. In fact, that has been the case all my life. I was always hanging out with the boys as a child. They were more fun and simple. It wasn't until I hit puberty that I started hanging out with the girls, and boy did I hate them. They were so petty, so catty, always had conflict and drama, no peace, no fun. They were just awful. Male healthcare workers were always nicer to me than female healthcare workers (especially gynecologists), and all of these men were white and straight yet super empathetic.

Women and gays were always jealous of me and went out of their way to hurt me when I was literally just sitting or standing there (especially the wives of cheating, straying husbands). Straight men, overall, were the one group who complimented me the most, admired me the most, and were the most respectful. There is no such thing as pretty privilege when you are hated by half the population for just being better-looking. Men also are more laid back than women, more humorous than women, more fun, less ridiculous, talk little (which I love), less self-centered, let minor things roll off their shoulders, and more rational, practical, logical, and less emotional. I don't want drama, hassle, and bullshit at every turn. I love and appreciate simplicity, and men offer that. Women are more emotional than men. Of course, they are; they are the incubators of primates. They must be. Not that men aren't emotional at all, but women are MORE so.

Under normal circumstances, I prefer a man's company. I find men to be calmer than women and less excitable. If I can, I usually request male doctors. I prefer white male doctors. Yep, overall, they treat me better, and I am statistically more than likely to get a white male doctor anyway. In my experience, white men have behaved more like gentlemen to me than any other race in this country. A white man is most likely to hold the door open for me. Even when I do not look attractive, a random white man will still be a gentleman. Even when I had a bad teenage attitude, the white male cops were very patient with me, and I was in the wrong while driving. I was driving like a typical, underdeveloped frontal lobe teenager. I cannot say the same about men of color being gentlemen, though. (Have there been bad apples within the white group? Of course. You have a 50/50 chance of meeting bad apples. However, these are my experiences overall). We should be encouraging chivalry, not discouraging it. In summation, men do have a lot to offer to the world. Their existence came about for a reason, to diversify DNA, and that they did. There is also a spiritual reason why they exist. They are needed to balance energy. They are here to balance karma. They are the Yang to our Yin, and there is no world without them.

"Peace Be With You, And Also With You"

Before you decide to hurt someone else, remember that pain comes back to you. Yes, I do believe in karma, not just as a punishment but as a chance to change for the better. You learn, through pain and, what not to do to others. When I see or hear news of tragic events that happen to people, I always think to myself, what was their karma? What did they do in this life, or the former life, to experience this event now? How do you know Ted Bundy's victims weren't his enemies in a previous life? We all are guilty of hurting someone, whether intentionally or not. Who is right? Who is justified in their actions? Be careful whom you hurt because you just might get that back. We should try to minimize pain on this planet; even though pain is inevitable, why do you contribute to more? Pain is here to teach us. It is here to teach us to do better, to teach us to minimize pain, and to become closer to God.

I often go out of my way to teach people valuable lessons. This is my fate. I teach people what not to do to not only me, but to others as well. Humans respond to consequences, both negative and positive. When they experience a negative consequence, they are least likely to repeat that same behavior. This dumb, fat broad on TikTok said to me that people learn through education, and we should give them second chances. Women with their damn second chances bullshit. Negatory Ghost Rider. They don't learn through education. If they did, everyone in the USA would have changed all their behaviors by now. People have and always will learn through the consequences of their behaviors. I see it in life, and I learned this as a psychology major. Give them an incentive to produce a desired behavior, and they will display that desired behavior. This is why, from what I heard, the California government gave crack addicts 40k to agree to sterilization. Give someone an incentive to stop an undesired behavior, and they will stop. It's that simple. This is why we have laws, rules, regulations, and all consequences. I find most people do not like to get into conflict. Why? Because of, you guessed it, consequences. Whether it's an arrest or a murder, the result is the same.

How do you discourage people on welfare from having kids? Stop giving them welfare and only give it to people who are child-free or agree to sterilization. America ain't ready for that. Humans don't listen to reason most of the time, and you must introduce the uncomfortable for the greater good. It's that easy. Either you want peace on the planet, or you don't. Make up your mind. You must make those tough choices to get the reward. You must sacrifice to gain. Nothing good comes easy. What are you willing to sacrifice to receive? You give to get into this world. Nothing comes without a cost. Even love has its conditions. You would not keep being nice to someone over and over if all they did was give you pain. Eventually, whether in this life or the next, you will stop doing that without receiving that kindness in return. I rarely go out of my way to help people. That doesn't always fair well.

This brings us to the idea of privilege. What makes you so special that you feel you are deserving of more? Who said that? In what life rule book did it state you should get what other people get, people whom you perceive as having it better? Why should someone who seems to have a better life than you, destroy their life for you to be happy? How do you know you aren't privileged yourself? How do you know you don't have an advantage over someone else? Those who make you jealous are not responsible for your pain. Take your complaints to Human Resources in Heaven. Instead of trying to take down someone you are jealous of, why don't you improve your life and yourself? I refuse to allow those who suffer so greatly to ruin any happiness for the rest of us. I do everything in my power to give these poor souls great learning lessons.

I see it a lot and hear about it a lot about how jealous these so-called marginalized groups are of others. We all experience pain no matter how sucky or great our lives appear to be to anyone. Why are you adding to others' pain just because your life sucks? These marginalized groups have absolutely no empathy for others at all. They are not the peace-loving people they claim to be. They are quite evil and selfish. If you are a white person or a person who is a member of a group that is accused of having it so much better than others, and you are reading this, please, whatever you do, do not help people who seek to take you down. Do not feel pressured or obligated to minimize your "privilege" because others are less fortunate. Do not let them guilt trip you into making your life a living hell. I recommend segregating from those who suffer greatly. Your presence in their lives could hurt you. Do not allow these libbies to make you feel guilty about your success and happiness. Do not allow them to take away your peace when you obviously have earned it. You, unlike them, have good karma. Please, fight back on these liberals and put them in their places. You have my permission, as a biracial woman who has had a challenging life herself, to give them back what they have given you.

I do not ever want to take your happiness away. I may wish I had some things you have, but it would be cruel, ungodly, and unfair of me to try to make you feel ashamed for having a great life. I want people to do well on this planet. There is so much suffering; it's nice to see some people happy, and 9 times out of 10, these happy people will always treat me better. Those who are unhappy treat me like shit. I would rather surround myself with certain groups of people who are less likely to commit a crime against me than those who have little in life and little to lose. Those who have next to nothing do not care about hurting others, and they would jump at the chance to take anyone down, especially those whom they perceive as "having it all." Look at all these people who are jealous of the 1% they talk about so much. Yeah, it sucks. Seems unfair, right? Unless you have spiritual beliefs, you will never find peace with your reality. Unless you believe in a greater purpose or a bigger reason, you will never draw closer to the Light. I'm pissed off too, but I believe in something better, something more meaningful. A lot of the time, there are things you can do to improve your life. You have that freedom here in the U.S.A.

Don't make your problems other people's problems. Learn to make peace with your past, your present, and your future before it's too late. I am so happy I voted for Trump (twice, actually), and I am happy there are plans to stop this madness. You people have the power of choice. You can make choices that would make your lives better. The government doesn't force you to have sex, which could lead to pregnancy, disease, and heartbreak. The government doesn't force you to have children while you're poor and unmarried. The government was not the one who abandoned you, abused you, or brought you into this world. Your families and your loved ones were the first humans to make your life a living hell. They also had choices. They had a choice to make their lives better - in a country where we have some advantages - so that future generations don't have to suffer. However, they made bad choices, and they have all the power in the world to choose differently. Take up your gripes with them. Get mad at your community, your parents, not Bob who lives in a million-dollar home. Learn from your family's generational trauma and karma, and do not repeat the same mistakes. I did not give birth to potentially deformed organisms that could have ruined us all. I did not have kids in poverty with little education. I did not marry an asshole of a man, or worse, give a shitty man kids. All these things make all of our lives worse. Fuck capitalism! Close your goddamn legs.

So, you want compassion, you say? Don't feel entitled to it, but I recommend extending that compassion as well to those whom you think have advantages over you. Otherwise, I am gonna be just as tough on you as I would be with them. I am not God, ask God for that unconditional love and empathy. I am not required to give it to you. I have every right to hold you accountable for having the freedom to be a piece of shit, often without facing consequences. I 1000% believe in law and order. I want peace. In fact, I wish Reagan did not close those mental hospitals, we fucking need them. Not everyone belongs in the community, as they can hurt others and often do. I do not believe in inclusion. Not everyone can function properly in the world. I do not give a shit about the government as much as I care more about my daily life, where I am faced with potential criminals every day. You people will destroy me faster than any government entity or any leader whom you think is a dictator. Ever think maybe Trump is right about a few things? If you really wanted peace, you would be on board with the death penalty for all 50 states. Currently, most red states have the death penalty and a couple of blue ones. You complain about the red, yet the red is tough on crime. Do you freaks want more violent offenders or fewer? I mean, come on.

There is no weird conspiracy theory against certain groups. The reality is certain groups do a lot of damage. This is happening. How is it that you even get to a point where you are arrested and then convicted? I have had crimes committed against me by the very same people you claim are marginalized. Not my fault their lives suck; it doesn't give them the right to take the rest of us down with them. Furthermore, they need to learn how to accept their fate. This is between them and God, not me, not the rest of us. There is a group, who often become defensive over criticism, very needed criticism. They are often angry, vengeful, combative, argumentative, confrontational, OMG, basically all of the above. They are often a very hateful group. They have all the power in the world to make their community better if they stick together. They have all the power in the world to relocate back to Africa and help their fellow man.

They have all the power in the world to NOT have kids with other races, not have sex, not have kids out of wedlock, not commit crimes, not abuse their children and animals, not hate all light skin and all white people, oh and not complain about situations they have the power to change. You want change? BE THE CHANGE. They have serious BAD KARMA dating back to the beginning. They have a history of hurting their own kind, hurting others, and now complaining that those bad choices came back to haunt them. They continue to spread negativity throughout the country and will soon experience the repercussions of that. They, like many humans, often never learn their lesson the first time. Oh, but they will. The reality is the slaves of yesteryear were the miscreants of Africa (Like European immigrants who were also the poor of their countries). These weren't the crème de la crème of humans. These weren't the elites in Africa who were sold by their own kind. They were criminals, the poor, the downtrodden of their own countries. Don't allow the average black person to convince you they came from royalty. Yeah, okay, that's not even logical. Most people aren't wealthy in the past or the present. You are not Queens and Kings. You are "Pookie" and "Le' Shandra."

We will not allow anyone in this country to make our experiences worse just cause your lives suck. This includes those trannies who think they're women. You have no right to destroy athletic careers because you have some mental issue the medical community refuses to address. I have stopped you from becoming a bigger problem. I did have help, too. I am super happy most people voted for Trump. I am happy there are some people who are rational and have common sense. Funny how everyone hates men, yet men have been big supporters of women when it comes to this trans bullshit occupying female spaces. I am so grateful for these men who respect women and their nature.

Yeah, men have many flaws, but guess what? So do women. I will not allow women to receive special treatment just because they have a pussy. It is unfair and unjust when men fall behind. I have no problem with the feminism of the past. I do have a problem with the feminism of the present. I did not vote for Hilary for one big reason: she wanted to give mothers special treatment in custody cases. Oh, hell no. I feel parents should have joint, physical custody, and the process for men should not be difficult or costly. Unless either parent is super horrible, I see no reason for one parent to receive full custody. It should be shared. Both parents can work and split the expenses. Men, or anyone, should not pay alimony. If you are no longer contributing to the marriage, you should no longer benefit from it. I do not believe in alimony. Men suffer greatly financially in a divorce, and that is unfair. Women are PARTLY responsible for the breakdown of the marriage. Why should you get anything unless you personally contributed financially? You should be preparing for marriage. Get your money right before you get married, just in case you divorce. The work you did as a wife was paid for by being fed, housed, clothed, etc. These are all things you would have paid for anyway if you were getting paid at a regular job. You chose children, and now you want to get paid to take care of your own kids? That's fucking insane. Why did you have kids then?

You people are not special, and you never will be. I will humble you within two seconds if you think for a moment the world revolves around you. Try not to be self-centered and truly "love thy neighbor as thyself." Recently, I got into an argument with some black dude about what it means to be biracial. I told him, "You people love claiming biracial people as one of your own when it benefits you (Halle Berry, Obama), but other times, they're not 'black enough.' So, which is it?" Are biracial people black or white, according to black people? If a biracial person says they're black, and a black person disagrees, whose side do you take? See how conflict happens when you are an irrational primate? Race should not be a social construct if people disagree about who is what. I can identify as white and have white people disagree with me and even get angry about it. So, who is right? Me, or white people? It is best to go by your actual genetic ancestry for racial identification. This madness is crazy. Race is a reality, not in your imagination. The facts are I am biracial. I have proof of this. It doesn't matter what your overemotional mind thinks of me; what matters are the facts. Cultural experiences or not, it doesn't matter. You can still be accused of appropriating someone's culture. You see why this is ridiculous?

Anyway, this guy did not like hearing the truth and became defensive, which is very common with black people when you offer constructive criticism. He said that I was playing the victim. HA! That's like the pot calling the kettle black, quite literally. LOL. So here are my responses to him and another comment I made on a different reel:

> **stankpuzz** 8s
> @danimal_95 on the contrary black ppl play the victim card 24/7 . You have it backwards . You're projecting my man . Maybe ppl are beneath me . I take responsibility for my actions choices and my role in events surrounding me . You ppl do not . You're very emotional like a woman. Which is common with black men . No masculinity whatsoever . Real men own up to their crap and control their emotions. If you flip over words I can't imagine how you handle a real challenge. lol 😂 we pity you people . By the way by 2050 the black wealth will reduce down to 0 . Sounds like a personal failure of your own community. Good luck with that "brotha" 😂
>
> Reply

Comments

stankpuzz 35s
I've observed behavior too. Coming from black people : they lack empathy for others but expect empathy from others . They are aggressive violent angry combative argumentative sexist the men hate women hurt their own women at alarming rates the men abandon their children the women and men have kids out of wedlock . This group is the poorest in the country the least educated the most problematic and they want revenge and often seek revenge against everyone non black . The feeling is mutual buddy . Ever think you're the problem and not everyone else ?

Reply

Now, I would not have been so mean if he did not come at me nasty. The comment he was responding to was innocent; however, he became too emotional and thought he "did something." Yes, I have troll accounts online. This is a part of how I do my research for my writing. I acquire information, make observations, and conduct experiments, often using myself as one of the subjects. And yes, my name on Instagram is "StankPuzz." LOL. Hilarious. And, hey, look at my sexy pic. LOL. Anyway, this black dude, who appeared to have a much better financial situation than I have (oh, the "privilege!"), called me a racist. LOL. Really? I have zero power over you. If anything, because of Obama and Biden, you have more power over me.

Let me enlighten you on a little secret: we are all prejudiced towards different groups. Women are prejudiced against men, men against women, whites against blacks, blacks against whites, and so on. Did you know that it is scientifically accurate to say that prejudice is normal and natural? ([How to Work with the Bias in Your Brain](#)-greatergood.berkley.edu) Different groups throughout history have not gotten along. Even within the same racial group, there is conflict. If a human being experiences patterns of behaviors or trends with a certain group, it's normal and rational to develop beliefs about that group. This is how we survive. If people do not want stereotypes about them, then they should alter their behaviors so that others can have a positive experience. It's understandable some people will be turned off by black people if many people report their encounters with black people as being negative. We are not talking about one or two people; we are talking about MANY people having repeated, negative experiences. The responsibility to rectify these issues is on the group whose actions and behaviors are deterring others from engaging with them. Remember I said there are other people in the world who surround you? "No man is an island." It is common that black people (and even some other groups) refuse to assimilate into the larger, main American culture. They are holding onto this "blackness" they speak about so often. This is what happens when we have diversity and no unity. We all must be on the same page, culturally, so that we can have a harmonious existence. If you refuse, then you should segregate or relocate out of the U.S.A.

If you want to live in America, fine, then you must behave like the majority group and think like them. Otherwise, we will never get along. We will always have conflict. I saw a black woman on Instagram who sued a hospital she worked at, and she won. She claimed the black mothers giving birth were treated horribly. I hear this a lot. So, I looked up why black mothers experience higher mortality rates than other groups of mothers. (I do not deny some racism. But I often wonder if it is as common as it is portrayed. Again, you have a 50/50 shot of running into bad apples). What I found out about black mothers is that they tend to be unhealthy people. They are also the least likely to seek prenatal care. Obviously, they are also less educated and more than likely to be poorer ([Black Maternal Mortality-The Elephant in the Room - PMC](#)). All of these realities will 1000% contribute to higher mortality rates. In addition to that, as someone who used to work in healthcare, I can tell you it is a common practice - partly due to insurance companies refusing to pay - that patients are treated like commodities. White mothers go through similar outcomes, in terms of only being allowed to stay at the hospital for a very short time after giving birth or certain treatments or medicines these mothers are given. The white elderly experience the same. My white parents, who are elderly, have complained about the subpar healthcare they have experienced in hospitals. In addition, because of Democratic policies, the elderly cannot even receive enough painkillers for their pain. Do you want to make the elderly suffer more so that people who are responsible for their drug addictions do not abuse painkillers? Address drug addiction directly. We all shouldn't suffer because of these drug addicts. So, this is an American issue that is not rooted in race at all.

I would also like to add an important concept, that I just touched on before. Black people, as I said before, have certain behaviors and attitudes that are unique to their sub-culture, like a lot of groups. Again, some of their behaviors are off-putting and deter people from interacting with them or deter people from dealing with them. I can see these behaviors contributing to the experiences black people have with white people or other groups. This also applies to mentally ill patients, who often feel they have physical problems that are not there. I have had panic attacks before that really feel like something is wrong with my body. Anxiety manifests in the body, and it often makes you think there is something else wrong. No, it's just anxiety. I understand why healthcare professionals become frustrated with mentally ill patients. A lot of people also feel frustrated with the black Americans. Even other black groups who are not originally from America have these opinions about black Americans. HealthScare has a lot of problems, but its main problem has nothing to do with race. We are all suffering from our American HealthScare system.

I see why people are reluctant to accept DEI initiatives. Number one, if you try to guilt-trip people, attack them, blame them, they are naturally going to fight back against your efforts. Your behaviors will backfire, which is what America is experiencing now. According to an interview with Dr Frank Dobbin, a sociologist, "DEI training is ineffective, causing more discriminatory behavior. You alienate people when you seek to shame them." I looked up some information about DEI. The left claims standards are not lowered to allow these marginalized groups into universities or companies. This is incorrect (Report Reveals Just How Much the DEI Complex Has Infiltrated Medical Education More Diversity, Lower Standards — Minding The Campus). In fact, courses have been changed to make them less strenuous for POC, who tend to have lower grades and lower IQs. I looked up the IQs of Black Americans compared to White Americans, and I found out that black people have 75% of the white person's IQ level. This is not good, and its reason is not due to genetics but it is due to socioeconomic factors. So, to get black people on an even playing field, black people must personally take the initiative to improve their socioeconomic status. Why would you want a surgeon to perform surgery on you who has gotten where they are without merit? That's fucking dangerous, people. It is not up to white people or the government to treat you like babies. You have personal choices. In 2025, you have privilege. Black people are still allowing themselves to be bound by chains, refusing to let go. Seriously, you're not slaves. Why are you acting like one? I read an article written by a Medical Director who spoke about his personal experiences with DEI (Medical Education Is Infected with DEI — The James G. Martin Center for Academic Renewal). He got fired for speaking up. Below is another article that said standards were, in fact, lowered for POC med students. Essential standards for becoming a doctor. How insane is this? There were several testimonies about how colleges were saturated with this "inclusion" rhetoric, which includes other "marginalized" groups like the disabled, the rainbow mafia, etc. People were overwhelmed by this tyranny disguised as a peace-loving inclusion, diversity, and love for all things. It was shoved down their throats, and they were told they were the evil villains. Several courses about diversity and biases were required for students, and some said, "All you need is one course on the topic." These DEI courses took precedence over the essential courses needed to become a doctor or obtain a PhD., in addition to standards being lowered. The insanity is outrageous. You see why people voted for Trump?

The *Free Beacon* noted that the med school's *U.S. News & World Report* ranking had dropped from 6 to 18 since 2020, and the story shared leaked data showing students' poor performance on their shelf exams. (These evaluations are used as preparation for the national licensing exams that every M.D. recipient must pass before they can practice medicine in the United States.) According to Sibarium, almost one-quarter of the class of 2025 had failed at least three shelf exams, while more than half of students in their internal-medicine, family-medicine, emergency-medicine, or pediatrics rotations had failed tests in those subjects at one point during the 2022–23 academic year—and those struggles led many trainees to postpone taking their national licensing exams. "I don't know how

TO READ THIS STORY, **SIGN IN** OR ✕
START A FREE TRIAL.

professor told him. "Faculty are seeing a

I have worked in the business of helping the disabled get jobs. I have had a client who received accommodation after accommodation; managers bent over backward for her - only for her to then continue to complain repeatedly about nonsense. She was never happy. She complained about me and other people who worked with her. She had mental health issues; although unfortunate for her, it is unfair for us to have to tolerate that. You wind up slowing things down, nothing gets done, businesses lose money, and it affects work morale and productivity.

This inclusion agenda is not a good thing. I see why companies are reticent about hiring the disabled or anyone who has behavior problems. Not everyone is qualified to do certain jobs. Just because you want to do a certain job does not mean you are good at it. It doesn't mean you will be useful or helpful. You must discriminate. Sometimes it is necessary to discriminate to make life more manageable. We naturally discriminate for survival. For instance, some of us choose to eat healthily so that we don't suffer and die. We are "discriminating" against bad foods. That's necessary for our lives to be more harmonious. I feel the same way about this DEI topic. You must meet people halfway, at least. If you approach them with the attitude, "You're the bad guy," they'll just say, "Fuck off," and won't consider your feelings at all. You need to lead with love, not hate, which is what the liberal left is doing by leading with hate. You also must, you know, not be a psycho and think someone who has a lowered IQ or bad grades should be a doctor.

I do not blame companies for not wanting to hire parents either, especially women who have kids or who are pregnant. As I mentioned earlier about mothers, they take time from work, leave extra work for the rest of us to do, etc. It makes sense to me, and it is perfectly reasonable to not want them in a work atmosphere. This is the reason why I say the American, human primate has now become so overemotional that it is affecting our ability to maintain any peace or normalcy. It's insane. This overemotional movement is primarily led by women, and this is exactly how women affect society; this is how women destroy lives.

I will give you another example of a deaf woman working at a grocery store. I tried to order a cake for someone's birthday; this deaf woman could NOT HEAR ME. I screamed, I yelled, OMG, it was hurting my own ears. Of course, what happened? My cake got screwed up. She fucked up the order, and the birthday party was ruined. The store gave me a refund and sent me an apology note. This deaf woman was not meant to be taking orders. COME ON, BE REASONABLE. She could mop floors in the back or do something else. Taking orders requires your ability to hear!!! Are you people insane or what? The manager said, "Well, it's illegal for us to discriminate." LOL, You're not doing a bad thing by placing this deaf woman in a job task she is ABLE to do. Let her clean the toilets. Even then, she needs to hear somewhat. Where is her hearing aid? Somebody should purchase her hearing aid. You know what, though? I know the disabled so well that there would be times this deaf woman would REFUSE to wear it. Some of these people do not want help, and they fight you for doing things that would benefit them.

Back To People Not Getting Along

Take the indigenous, for example, there were several tribes in this continent who had a history of battles, conflicts, and problems. Why? Because of difference. The three tribes in my state all fought against each other; two tribes were traitors and sided with the British. The other tribe (I have more respect for) stood their ground and fought against the other two tribes and the Europeans. They lost, obviously, but if all three of these tribes stuck together, this state would not even be a reality. The Europeans would not have "colonized" this area at all. Many indigenous tribes were quite evil and often participated in black magic to hurt others or get revenge. This concept of the natives being holier than thou is super nuts and not based on reality. We have evidence of their battles with their own people (Early History portal.ct.gov/about/earlyhistory.com).

Africans also have a history of doing wrong not just to each other but also to other nations (Five Major African Wars and Conflicts of the Twentieth Century | Norwich University - Online 7 Influential African Empires | HISTORY. Moors and Saracens in Europe: estimating the medieval North African male legacy in southern Europe - PMC). They are human primates like everyone else, who can do bad like everyone else. They are not innocent, and they also have some bad karma. I say this because none of us are as innocent as these marginalized groups claim to be. Your people have a history of doing wrong – not just the "colonizers." Your people are also prejudiced. Black people, when given a little bit of power, 100% abuse that power, hurting, you guessed it, white people or other non-black groups. Like I said in my comment, black people want revenge, and lately, they have been feeling a little too confident trying to get that revenge.

Because of these differences, I feel segregation is a good thing. It would bring more peace and minimize conflict if groups would stick to their own. We have that already. Asians and Indians are so successful in the U.S.A. because they stick to their own kind. They help their own kind, they marry their own kind, they have kids with their own kind, and they stay the fuck away from other groups. I have come across tons of black folks who have had it better than whites. Give me a break. Indians and Asians right now are doing better economically than whites. (How Black, Hispanic, Asian, White households compare in wealth | Pew Research Center) Furthermore, you are responsible for your own community. If you can't get along with your own people, that's not the rest of the world's fault. You have the power of choice. You are no puppet. The global majority? Sure, but not the global power. African elites hurt their own people, and I do not see black celebrities or politicians saving Nigeria or Chicago right now. Speaking of Nigeria, look at all these BILLIONAIRE NIGERIANS:

Aliko Dangote

Africa's richest man and Nigeria's wea
with a fortune from Dangote Cement
largest cement producer. 🔗

Mike Adenuga

A telecommunications magnate and 1
Globacom, Nigeria's second-largest r
network operator. 🔗

Abdulsamad Rabiu

A Nigerian billionaire. 🔗

Femi Otedola

Chairman of Geregu Power Plc and F
holdings. 🔗

Folorunsho Alakija

A prominent businesswoman and phi
chair of Famfa Oil. 🔗

Tony Elumelu

Chair of Heirs Holdings, the United Ba
and Transcorp, and founder of the To
Foundation, which focuses on youth ᵉ

Jim Ovia

Founder of Zenith Bank, one of Nigeri

 🔒🔍 nigerian billionaires

A simple Google search will show you the net worth of all Democrats, celebrities, and leaders of the world. California is suffering right now as I type this. But, hey, at least Gavin Newson is living large, right? Why ain't these rich BLACK PEOPLE helping their fellow black people? Why is Nigeria suffering at the same time these Nigerian billionaires are living large? Your problems aren't racism. It never was. Your problems are your own people. Blacks are the least successful. You gotta ask yourself why? What is the objective reason? If black people spent less time complaining about racism and more time trying to make their own community better, they would acquire more wealth and power on this planet. They would be able to successfully compete with other groups. Right now, America and China have Africa by the balls. When black folks get that money, they don't do shit for their own kind. This is the total opposite of what these other groups, who are successful, do. Black folks would rather hurt each other instead of helping each other. You lose power when you play the victim. You are giving your power away to white people by blaming them for your own personal failures. Even Africans who migrate to the USA are doing better than black Americans. Why? Look at Haitians. Plenty wrong with the Haitian culture (they love doing black magic too, yet none of it is working; they are still suffering). However, the one thing they are is very industrious. I've never met a lazy Haitian. I've never heard them make excuses to blame white people or anyone else for their problems. You know what else? They stick to their own kind and help their own kind. They operate as a group, like many immigrants who migrate to the U.S.A.

In America, we operate as individuals. Family doesn't matter. The group doesn't matter. It's the reason for so many problems we experience. When you stay in this state of victimhood, you will always be a victim. Your life will never change. You will live an endless karmic cycle of misery. That's fine if that's what you want. However, you absolutely have no right to make your problems our problems. You have no right to take the rest of us down into your misery. This is why I say to white people, segregate as much as possible. Stay away from other groups. It is the best way to have peace here, in the U.S.A. I feel segregation is very useful. Black people would never have to experience racism again if they lived in their own country around their own people. This is why I tell them, "Go back to Africa." Not as an insult, but a very great suggestion. I have already seen black people relocate to Ghana, and Ghana is offering free citizenship for blacks. It's already happening. Africa owes you since Africans were the first to hurt you. You should go back and get your reparations from Africans. Or you can sue those wealthy people directly who truly profiteered off your backs. The average taxpayer isn't responsible. Go back to the homeland and make your community and your lives better. They could use your help over there. Don't blow it.

It's natural for like groups to prefer their own. It works the same with relationships. We tend to surround ourselves with people who are like us - similar opinions, interests, and careers. This works with marriages, too. Couples with similar incomes and career paths choose each other. Another big reason is proximity. We tend to get into connections with people who are physically close to us - people we covet every day. Makes logical sense, right? Makes sense, and it's scientifically true, that compatibility is necessary for connections to work for the long term. Even with some differences, you need a common ground to get along. This is what would bring more peace. This is how we would better get along. Maybe only black cops should go into black communities. That way, black people would have to blame their own people. Black banks, black hospitals, and black schools would improve the experiences of the black community. If you can't accomplish that in the U.S.A, please feel free to leave.

The Entitled, Spoiled Brat Of A Human

I never met the most entitled group of fucks more than human primates. My lord, the amount of people who feel entitled to anything and everything, especially without earning it is incredible. This feeling of entitlement isn't exclusive to any one group of people. ALL humans experience this feeling of entitlement at some point during their lives. We start out as children, and children are the most entitled bunch I've ever seen. The number of dispassionate humans I've come across, who were members of various groups is appalling. Who died and made you God? You are not special. This planet can survive without you. It survived the Ice Age, Wars, pollution, etc., and it can overcome your simple, dumb ass. We need wars, famine, and alike to keep the population down. It is practical and rational to have a manageable human population. Climate change is gonna happen no matter what, but the mere existence of humans contributes to that exact change ([Are humans causing or contributing to global warming? | NOAA Climate.gov](#)).

Remember when I mentioned that story about the rude Mother? Well, I was at Subway when this happened. For those who have been hiding under a rock for the last 30 years, Subway is a sandwich chain restaurant, that serves sandwiches, chips, cookies, and drinks, back to my story. I was at Subway, and this dumb, white trash broad had about 5,000 kids with her, along with the grandparents. Her son was running around the place, causing mayhem, ran into me, and almost tripped me. I said to this dumb broad, "Your son just ran me over!" This chick replied, "My son has special needs!" with her snotty attitude. I clapped back and said, "That's not my problem. If you can't handle it, don't have kids." Then, I turned to the grandparents and said, "You're the grandparents. You should know better!" I walked out of Subway. I was majorly pissed! How dare she feel entitled to space, disturb the peace, and inconvenience other people because her little world is screwed up. That's 100% selfish of her and anyone like her to bother other people. It is her job, as the mother, to watch her child. Not my kid, not my problem. If you're that much of a lazy primate and can't learn how to handle Autistic kids, why did you breed? That is your job to do whatever it takes to teach your kids, help them function within a normal society, and help them live a quality life.

Like I said before, I don't believe in inclusion at all. Not everyone can function properly, like the average person. This event about the Autistic mother is a great example. Not everyone can be trusted. Not everyone receives proper supervision. Certain people should have their own corner of the globe, their own society, their own country. Why should the rest of us suffer just because we're suffering? That's self-centered of you; so selfish and barbaric for you to take up space and hurt others just by your behaviors and actions. This brings me to this point: The parents today do not discipline their children at all. Then you people wonder why kids commit crimes or become addicted to drugs. You folks let your kids grow up like weeds to fend for themselves. No structure, no guidance, no supervision. Then you wonder why they get kidnapped. Sorry, but you should be sterilized.

The Rainbow Mafia

I touched on homosexuality earlier, and I wanted to provide real-life events and people to support my conclusions about gays, women, and men. All my life, I have encountered negative, aggressive gay men. In fact, I find gay men to be more aggressive and nastier than straight men. Gay men are still men, and they are just as masculine as straight men; for the women who like gay men, you like them because they don't see you as a threat. Gay men, who are now probably trans today, have always seen me as a threat. I was super feminine and very attractive. Gay men are obsessed with straight men. Gay men are jealous of straight women. They are jealous because we are the yin to the straight man's yang. One of my stories is about a gay man whom I tried to befriend. I said to myself, "Mary, give the gays a chance; maybe your theories are wrong."

Nope. Of course, with my luck, I ran into a toxic gay. This gay dude, we will call him Peter, proved my theories right, and he only solidified my disgust for gay men. Peter, like a lot of gay men I have known over the years, was obsessed with this straight guy who had a girlfriend. Peter made comments like, "I'm coming after your men, ladies." Peter would insult this poor girl he didn't even know personally. This straight guy made it clear that he was straight and had a girlfriend. Peter did not care, and he continued to pursue this straight guy. Peter purposely sought to hurt women because of his sick, sexually perverse mind. A mind that is mentally ill. I could not stand it anymore, so I told Peter off, and he blocked me from Snapchat. Like I said before, the biggest misogynists are gay men and women. That is proof right there. I have never heard a straight guy admit to going out of their way to hurt another woman. Straight men usually hurt out of passion - the heat of the moment - rarely plotting and planning like women and gays. I also noticed Peter would seem pissed off every time I talked about my sexual attraction to men or how the vibe between me and so and so was so intense. He was jealous, and this is the reason why gay men are only friends with women they don't find to be a threat. Gay men do not provide that part of the balance of energies; they instinctively know that. They are confused. They crave being a woman so that they can feel some balance within their soul. They feel out of balance being gay. Two men and two women are a lack of harmony. This is why so many gay relationships do not last, nor are they functional. In addition to that, the DV rate is highest among lesbians and gays versus straight couples. This includes bisexuals. So, in other words, the DV rate, altogether, is highest within the rainbow mafia group. Bisexuals seem to be the most common victims. This is why I say it is best for bisexuals to date only other bisexuals. I feel they will be least likely to run into issues when they date each other. Compatibility, remember? It's inaccurate to say most heterosexual relationships experience IPV. About 35% of straight women and 29% of straight men report abuse by a partner. That is not most straight relationships. Women often act like IPV happens all the time, in most cases. It does not. Notice how the percentage of straight men experiencing abuse is close to the percentage of straight women experiencing abuse. (WP-2015-23-v4-Joyner-Gender-and-Stability-of-Same-Sex.pdf (bgsu.edu) Two Decades of Same-Sex Marriage in Sweden: A Demographic Account of Developments in Marriage, Childbearing, and Divorce | Demography (springer.com) Lesbian couples are significantly more likely to get divorced than gay men (thepinknews.com)) When Intimate Partner Violence Meets Same Sex Couples: A Review of Same Sex Intimate Partner Violence - PMC)

I have a theory as to why the research says women are more sexually fluid than men. So, in other words, women are more likely to be bisexual than men. Men are either gay or straight. Most victims of childhood molestation are females. I feel this childhood experience screws up a woman's sexuality. She might develop a sexual aversion towards men, unhealed. She will tolerate men's bad behavior and be drawn to the comfort and safety of a woman. A psychologist once told me she didn't realize how common childhood sexual molestation was until she became a therapist. Why are men sexually into children? From what I read, a lot of these pedophiles have low IQs. For those who do not have low IQs, the emotional/social part of their brains is damaged somehow, possibly during fetal development. This is why some pedophiles feel no remorse. They feel pedophilia is okay and normal to them. They have an inability to maintain adult social relationships; they are immature. Men are also biologically wired to become violent. It has something to do with survival.

Anyway, back to homosexuals, who have a higher dissolution rate than straight couples. Lesbians have the highest rate of relationship dysfunction than both gay men and straight couples. This is interesting and supports my theory. These women were meant to be straight, and they crave their yang. Two individuals who are both too emotional will not work. Lesbian relationships are volatile. It appears women are very problematic in interpersonal relationships. I thought they were masters of empathy and social interactions. Apparently not. And you say cis straight men are the problem. It's not bigotry if it's reality. The lesbians I have encountered throughout the years displayed nothing but garbage behavior. They were sexually aggressive towards me in very gross, disgusting ways. They also always seemed miserable; they had constant attitudes, like gay men. They thought just because they were women, they could get away with being disgusting. You thought wrong bitch. I was repulsed by them. Their behaviors were worse than straight men. If it weren't for women supporting these nasty behaviors, gay rights would not have gone this far to the point now: anything goes, and children are affected. We do not care if you are gay. Just keep it at your side of the fence. I stay out of your spaces; you stay out of mine. This brings me to the trans topic…

Much has been said about this trans phenomenon, but I want to add my two cents. A Swedish study said the suicide rate for trans-post-op increases after 10 years. This tells me something: there is some other variable causing them to feel like they are in the wrong body because even post-op, they're miserable, and it's not because of society's lack of acceptance, as the libs will try to convince you. A trans woman's brain is more similar to a cis man's brain than a cis woman's (Brain Sex in Transgender Women Is Shifted towards Gender Identity - PMC (nih.gov)). This research (possibly politicized due to the current political climate) suggests trans women are on some range between being a man or a woman but closer to being a man than a woman if that makes sense. Basically, due to biology, trans women are MEN. What the lefty nuts do not want to tell you is that male and female brains are more similar than different, with slight variations. So, brain patterns are not a great indication of gender (Massive study reveals few differences between men's and women's brains | ScienceDaily).

Gender should only be defined by our reproductive systems, by basic human biology and anatomy. We only have two options: male or female. Intersexed is rare and a variation of those only two options: male and female. Furthermore, intersex has some dominant sex system despite this combination. With that said, transwomen, who often threaten violence against women online just like any other man would, do not belong in female sports, female bathrooms, or female prisons. Female prisoners have already gotten knocked up by these trannies. In addition to that, trans in these female prisons are quite often harassing and assaulting women at very high rates. I thought cis men were the problem. Who is going to take care of these kids made by these trannies? Where are they gonna live? In foster homes, where they will fall victim to sex trafficking?

You people are sick and vile, and you need to create your own spaces and pay for those spaces yourself. Look, it must be torture to be so nuts that you can't stand your body. I feel for them, but that doesn't mean they have a right to negatively alter the world for the worse. Your issues are not mine, and you are not the majority. Martin Luther King once said, "A perfect society is one that both includes the needs of the individual and the needs of the group." THE NEEDS OF THE GROUP. It is wrong for America to only focus on individuals and not the entire group of individuals. Trans people have mental problems, and there must be some other form of treatment to manage their issues. Like a lot of women who choose a homosexual lifestyle after being molested as children, I also feel trans people have gone through similar experiences as children. It's awful and very unfortunate. So, let's address that instead of entertaining nonsense. By entertaining nonsense and not addressing childhood trauma, you're basically encouraging abusers to continue to abuse.

I would also like to mention some time ago, I was seeing a therapist, who was super liberal-like-far-left liberal. Her liberal beliefs were part of why I stopped seeing her. In addition to that, she said to me, one time, during a session, "You know, if you want to "transition," I can approve of that." WTF?! LOL. First of all, I was talking about something else, entirely different, during this time. Why did she mention this? What did it have to do with what I was talking about? Secondly, at what point did I ever say I wanted to be a man? LOL! I was so fucking surprised. I never told her, not once, that I felt like a man or I wanted to be one. Just because I happen to be drawn to men or have some affinity towards the masculine (my astrological chart says I have more masculine energy than feminine) doesn't mean I want a dick or nuts. Nuts are gross. LOL! OMG! Not only did I not express a desire to be a man, but I also happened to express to her my disgust for this trans agenda, and I also expressed how horrible it is for men to be in female spaces. There was a time I

120

called a trans woman a "he," and this therapist corrected me. LOL. How does a 'he' even identify as a 'she?' This therapist assumed. I was so fucking pissed that she corrected me. This dude has literal cock and balls, and you're calling HIM a woman? Anyway, I could not believe how EASY it was to receive approval from a therapist to transition in the United States, even if you DO NOT say you want to transition. I never said I felt like a man, nor did I say I wanted to be one in any way, shape, or form. What the fuck? This tells me this trans shit is major bullshit. These people are sick. They need help. They do not need to transition, especially since they can still be miserable afterward. Also, no one wants to mention those detransitioners at all. Like, why? Someone regretting their surgeries is super significant. I left this therapist and her liberal ideas for one reason. She was not helpful to me at all. I think people rely too much on therapists. At some point, you need to use the skills you have learned. What people really need is a connection. A connection to God. My life improved 90% after leaving therapy. Therapy made me miserable.

I have encountered a lot of white, trans women online, who not only resort to racial slurs when you challenge them (I thought you people were pro-black? LOL), but they also resort to physical threats of violence, just like any other MAN, no surprise. This small percentage of white men are very sick people, and they need a hospital, not body mutilation. Female college students have lost scholarships, ruining their athletic careers because of these trannies. These girls worked hard all their lives, and now all that hard work was for nothing. In fact, in my state alone, there was a major lawsuit by a group of college women against the state. The female athletes lost the suit, of course, because my state is super libby. God, I wanna puke. No surprise, my state was the first to even allow trannies into female prisons. How sickening is this? Yet, they have no death penalty for sex offenders in this state. They're basically saying, "Go right ahead and rape all you want, molest kids all you want, and if you put on a dress, you can have a buffet of ladies at your disposal when we lock you up."

Speaking of the rainbow crowd, here is a tidbit you might find interesting. There was some controversy not too long ago about the Newson bill that was passed, giving the rainbow pedophiles freedom to offend by not making them register as sex offenders. Straight pedophiles must register, but gay ones do not have to register; yet they call this an "anti-discrimination" law? In other words, if you penetrate a vagina, you must register. If you suck a cock, you do not have to register under a judge's discretion (We all know California judges will always side with the gays). So, once again, rainbow people receive special treatment, even when hurting children. The public will not know who a danger to their child is if a predator gets to roam free, free to molest more children. If you support this nonsense, OMG, I won't say it. I would get into big trouble if I did, but you know what I am thinking. You are on my shit list.

The Hypocritical, Liberal Woman

Now, this is just sex offender registration, and I am about to go deeper into the abyss by talking about the death penalty for child molesters. I was curious if any state in the U.S.A. gives the death penalty to pedophiles, so I looked it up. I found out a lot of interesting things when I did Google this horrid topic, and I am quite sickened by what I found out. Now, I know what you're thinking; she must be against the death penalty. Well, if you think that, you haven't been paying attention this entire time, and you're a fucking moron. This is what I admire about men as a collective. Men are willing to kill for the greater good. Men are willing to hunt so that their families are protected. Men are willing to sacrifice and make those tough choices so that we may live freely and happily. Women, on the other hand, wanna save every fucking piece of shit out there, even if it means these women would be hurt in the process. I hate Gavin Newson, but I LOVE Governor Desantis. Desantis is the Governor of the state of Florida, and he challenged the Supreme Court and passed a bill that gives pedophiles the death penalty ([Death Penalty for Child Sexual Abuse that Does Not Result in Death | Death Penalty Information Center](#)).

The Supreme Court justices, mostly Republicans, are considering changing current laws so that all molesters receive the death penalty, even if the victim/s don't die. Governor Desantis is a Republican, but more importantly, he is rational. Other states are following in his footsteps, and currently, only four other states allow the death penalty for child molesters. Guess what? All these states are RED states. These states are Oklahoma, South Carolina (which seems to be one of the toughest states when it comes to crime), Montana, and Louisiana. (By the way, a big reason Gov. Desantis opposed Critical Race Theory is that the rainbow people jumped onto the backs of black folks to push their agenda, only setting the liberal black person back decades. You liberals hurt yourselves when you align with the devil).

Now, let's dive deeper into the rabbit hole and briefly talk about your precious, demented - Devil worshipping Democrats. My Google research led me to information about sex trafficking. What I learned is that the Hippie Lovin Demos drag their feet when it comes to creating sharp penalties for sex traffickers. Alabama, a red state, leads the country on the toughest sentence for human trafficking (Alabama enacts 'toughest' human trafficking penalties in the U.S. - Yellowhammer News). Conversely, Colorado & Washington, blue states, have the lowest conviction rates for sex traffickers, yet the highest rates of sex trafficking crimes (Why convictions lag compared to sex trafficking reports in the PNW | Cascade PBS). What does this tell us? Well, your creepy, Joe Biden & The Boys support and encourage sex crimes, especially sex crimes against children. Guess what? You have been helping them along the way by voting Democrat. DUMB. DUMB. DUMB. One more time, DUMB. Your liberal media distract you with talk about anti-abortion laws (I support abortion, in some cases), but never mention this topic of sex crimes, which is way more important and is also a current national crisis. They distract you with talk about Trump, all the while, they are fucking you royally behind your backs. Wolves in sheep's clothing, my dear. And as God said, "Behold, I send you off as sheep amidst the wolves." Wolves, they are indeed. Remember I said women wanna give every garbage human a second chance? They sure do, and women are more than likely to vote Democrat. This is exactly how women affect the world negatively, destroying all our lives. This is what I should have mentioned to that TikTok girl I spoke about earlier when she said, "How do women destroy lives like men?"

You ladies complain about men raping and men molesting children, but you continue to vote Democrat. You are unwilling to support the death penalty when we could have fewer if any, male or female offenders. You should be fighting for the death penalty and not abortion. As I said before, some people do not belong on this Earth, and some people should not exist. We need to do what is necessary, and if these crappy primates see the severe consequences of sex crimes, they will 1000% change their behaviors. If the consequence were death, offenders would not molest or rape. We would have fewer bad guys and more of the good guys.

This brings me to a time I conducted another little social experiment using car, bumper stickers. I wanted to see the reactions I would get with a Hillary Clinton bumper sticker and a Trump bumper sticker. Before the Clinton & Trump election, I bought both stickers. I first placed the Hillary sticker on the car bumper. Well, not surprisingly, I received so many compliments from women, mostly white women and one black woman. When I placed the Trump sticker on my car bumper, I received compliments from all white men. I also encountered an aggressive ambulance driver just because I had a Trump bumper sticker on my car. I thought you libbies were inclusive, accepting, and loving. I thought the conservatives were the violent, aggressive ones. Hmmm… Anyway, both groups, who loved my bumper stickers seemed super excited once they saw the stickers, so excited, you would think they nutted right in their pants. It was interesting, and this experiment, along with the fact most female registered voters are Democrats, tells me women are to blame for what is going on in this country. Women vote based on emotion. Men vote based on logic. This is why I say women are MORE emotional than men. Abortion was the leading reason why women voted for Kamala when abortion is literally the least of our worries. There are several ways a woman can prevent pregnancy in the first place, and the primary reason for most abortions is inconvenience, not rape, incest, or the life of the mother, all of which are rare cases. If kids are an inconvenience, why aren't you using birth control? Why aren't you using condoms? Why are you having sex? Let's stop making excuses for irresponsible behaviors. This is when compassion for others can become a problem. You need to keep your feelings in check for the greater good. So, we can have normalcy and not chaotic, overemotional primates wreaking havoc. You need to have a rational, logical mind to have a harmonious, well-balanced society. The Democrats have been in power for a long time, but we changed that this 2024 election. We all worked our magic at that voting booth. When procedures fail due to miscarriages, it has nothing to do with the abortion laws, but it has everything to do with malpractice. Please stop being so dramatic.

The liberal woman is willing to vote for a female who stays married to a man who received a blow job in the Oval Office, but not a man who also had sexual relations while married. The liberal woman will chastise men with whom she is romantically intertwined for their bad behaviors but hate her daughters-in-law for chastising their sons for their bad behaviors. The liberal woman will act sweet and accepting to your face until you disagree with her politics. The liberal woman is pro-woman, pro-choice until you tell her you decided to become a stay-at-home mom. The liberal woman will call you a "pick me" when you challenge her way of thinking. The liberal woman will speak up against the injustice for those "marginalized" groups, but during an argument, she will be the first to engage in a racial tirade. Lastly, the liberal woman decries equality in relationships, expecting her romantic partner to meet her needs, all while refusing to meet his needs. The liberal woman is a joke.

Proud Misanthrope

This is what happens when a society does not have spiritual beliefs. They embrace the darkness. I have maintained a very sweet disposition (until you piss me off) all my life, despite challenges. How was I able to do this? It was my belief in a higher power that helped me along the way. All my life, I felt different, and at one point during my youth, I wanted to be a nun, but I eventually changed my mind. This doesn't mean I do not accept God into my life. It just means I am still and always will be a human primate, after all. I am giving into my primate desires. We all do. We can strive to become closer to God, but if you are a human on planet Earth, you will always be a sinner. We are not inherently good or bad; we are a work in progress, and we have a lot to learn.

"You can't always get what you want…you can get what you need! Alright." Rolling Stones. I told someone recently that there is no purpose to human existence. His response was, "Yes, there is. God needs us; we are His children." Nope. God is complete all by Himself, and He doesn't need us for anything. It's the other way around. We need Him. This guy, like a lot of humans I speak to felt that human beings are deserving of love, attention, time, etc. I said, according to whom? You? Who are you? What makes you deserving? An outsider might have a different perspective, especially if you hurt someone else; someone might say, "I hope that person dies. I hope they get run over by a truck. What an asshole." In your world, in your mind, you're deserving, but someone else might have a different thought, and that someone else might be right. All too often, humanity thinks way too highly of themselves. All too often, the human ego is way bigger than my fat ass, and that's a problem (not my fat ass, the human ego is a problem). We are all sinners, born sinners, and we will die sinners. None of us are deserving of anything. It is a gift to be on this planet. Be grateful. We are given a second chance. A chance for salvation. A chance to do better than we have done before.

It's not God's forgiveness you need; you need the forgiveness from those you have hurt. God doesn't judge you; you judge yourself. Hell isn't a place; it's a state of being, and you put yourself there. I believe in reincarnation (I have a mixture of beliefs ranging from Christian to Buddhism. Although I am not 100% on board with any religion), and I feel we keep coming back until we get it right and we do not have to come back anymore. The alternative to living on planet Earth would have been much worse. This is our purgatory. You are not special; you never have been, but you can work to become special. Is it challenging? Of course, and it's supposed to be challenging. It takes WORK to become special; it doesn't happen just because you exist. You must earn everything. Paradise is earned, not given. You must suffer, learn, and then grow. You experience pain so that you can understand better. You learn what not to do in the future. You also learn what to do in the future. The Old Testament is accurate. It may be scary, but contrary to what most believe, God also brings destruction for a reason. Without dark, you would not know light. Without pain, you would not know joy, nor would you appreciate it. You are being watched 24/7. Your behaviors are being recorded by the Spirit World.

For those who are Christian, I want to remind you that the Bible states that as a believer, you are responsible for your depiction of Christ. So, if you scare off a non-believer from God, you will be equally judged on the same level as the non-believer of Christ. In other words, if you want to lead others to God, you must first be of God. You must first be on your best behavior. You are supposed to represent God, and if you represent God in a negative light, you will be held accountable. Here is the quote from the Bible I am referencing:

Galatians 6:10 commands believers to "do good to all men" and to share the good news about Jesus Christ with non-believers.

1 Corinthians 5:12 says that it's not the responsibility of Christians to judge non-believers but rather to judge those who are inside the church who are sinning.

The Bible also says that Christians should be responsible for their actions towards others. For example,

Luke 10:30-37 says that Christians should be responsible for the way they act towards others.

1 Timothy 5:8 says that Christians should be responsible for the way they treat their families.

Now, there is such a thing as righteous judgment; however, my focus here is on Christians' behaviors. I never force my spiritual beliefs onto others. I speak in basic, human terms and understanding, and I often reference science to stay as objective and logical as possible. This is very important to do when trying to convince people of a higher power. You must speak their language. We are given the ability to be logical for a reason; there is value in that. We were given the ability to be rational for a reason. It helps us stay grounded. It helps us function as humans. It helps us keep our energy balanced. I often make the connection between science and religion because if you pay attention, there is a connection. Even astrology is connected to science. Famous serial killers' astrological charts indict their fate in becoming killers. Not ironically, science has analyzed their brains and indicated their propensity to kill. How interesting is that? More importantly, why were they created to kill? What is the spiritual reason for that? It is like a spider's web. We're connected to God, we're connected to Earth, and we are all connected to each other.

I have come across a lot of Christians who attend service weekly, but when they are out of the church building, they go back to being a piece of shit in their daily lives. And you wonder why non-believers question your authenticity. One Christian told me that the church is a hospital. Excuse me? If I wanted to attend a hospital, I would go to an actual hospital. Why would anyone choose to surround themselves with sickness? You're nuts. The church should be a holy place. A place of light energy, clean energy, pure energy, and not dysfunctional whatsoever. It is supposed to be a place of peace, and it is the one place you should make an effort to be on your best behavior. Why is it difficult for you to behave appropriately for one hour? This tells me there are some real-life, practical needs that are being neglected if you cannot control yourself in a church. In fact, being a practical, normal person is very important for spiritual growth. Remember Maslow's Hierarchy of Needs?

Eve, the first sinner, I am not surprised she fell for that apple. I used to think the story of Adam and Eve was sexist until I grew up and realized it makes sense the gender who is easily manipulated by a man would be easily manipulated by a simple snake. The devil showed Eve who he was, yet she decided to give in to temptation anyway. That means the power was in the woman's hands, and she gave that power away, and we all have been suffering ever since. It's not about fault or blame; it's about taking responsibility for one's own ROLE in any situation. What did you do to contribute? You, like anyone else, are not innocent. No one is innocent. You are, at your core, very flawed. You are a primate. You might be dressed up in a costume, but if you remain on planet Earth, you will always be an animal. You are nothing more than the "The Modern Ape."

THE END

www.ingramcontent.com/pod-product-compliance
Lightning Source LLC
Chambersburg PA
CBHW051210120626
46547CB00013B/1285